Dr. Simon Evans

*A Recipe for Feeding Your Child's Dreams
and Unlocking Their Maximum Brain Power*

New York

BRAIN FITNESS

© 2007 The Brain Code LLC. All rights reserved.

No part of this publication may be reproduced or transmitted in any form or by any mean, mechanical or electronic, including photocopying and recording, or by an information storage and retrieval system, without permission in writing from author or publisher (except by a reviewer, who may quote brief passages and/or show brief video clips in a review).

Paperback ISBN: 978-1-60037-235-3
Hardcover ISBN: 978-1-60037-236-0

Published by:

Morgan James Publishing, LLC
1225 Franklin Ave. Ste 325
Garden City, NY 11530-1693
Toll Free 800-485-4943
www.MorganJamesPublishing.com

Cover and Interior Design by:
Michelle Radomski
One to One Creative Services
www.creativeones.net

Brain Illustrations by:
Mindy Steffen
http://www-personal.umich.edu/~steffenm/

I dedicate this book to my wife, Marne and my kids Aidan and Kian.

They provide constant inspiration to reach out and add something positive to our world.

ACKNOWLEDGEMENTS

This book is the compilation of efforts from many people, some of whom don't even know they contributed.

First, my wife Marne has made this book possible with her unwavering support. Marne has stuck with me through the stress of graduate school and post-doctoral training, which required moving across the country and away from her close-knit family. She continues to stand by me while I move from a behind-the-scenes academic research role to one of reaching out to people in all walks of life. She has been a stable pillar who has taught me a great deal. She is an incredible mother and caring human being who I love very much. My kids, Aidan and Kian, are also partially responsible for this book. Parenthood is a life-long learning experience and they continually educate me.

My parents, Reg and Betty Evans, have also contributed to this book. They taught me at a very young age the value of following through and not quitting, which has been an invaluable tool in this endeavor. They have always supported me, even when they questioned my decisions.

Stepping from a world of academic science to one of private authoring is a big leap. I would not have known what to do without the coaching of Glenn Dietzel, John Paul and Deborah Micek, and Stephen Pierce.

I am also grateful to everyone that provided interviews, offered as downloadable recordings throughout the book: Dr. Alan Logan, Dr. Dean Miller, Chef Ann Cooper, Coach Cliff McCrath and Mr. Chick Moorman. Their insight and efforts to improve people's lives are inspirational to us all.

These pages represent all of my teachers, mentors and coaches in one way or another. It is impossible to know how the lack of any experience would have changed my course.

TABLE OF CONTENTS

Acknowledgements iii
Preface 1

Introduction

Chapter 1   Set It Up
            Feeding Dreams .7

Laying the Foundation of Physical Health

Chapter 2   Get It In
            Nutrition 17

Chapter 3   Work It Out
            Physical Activity .51

Chapter 4   Slow It Down
            Sleep and Relaxation 73

Building Creativity and Independence

Chapter 5   Soak It Up
            Learning Experiences 93

Chapter 6   Own It
            Creative Thinking 119

Chapter 7   See It to Believe It
            Dream Big Dreams 137

Finale

Chapter 8   Put It all Together
            Maximize Brain Power 155

About the Author 161

Claim Your Free Bonuses Today 163

PREFACE

What is Different About this Book?

I wrote this book because I see an alarming trend in today's society. Kids are losing their health and not reaching the potential that is their birthright. Some experts believe that today's youth could be the first generation to have a shorter life span than their parents. I hope to motivate parents to take action by clearly explaining the consequences of inaction. Unfortunately, in today's world the path of ill health is the default path. We must be proactive to overcome social trends and raise healthy children to set them up for the life of success that they deserve.

This book is for parents who feel lost in the sea of advice from medical professionals and the media. I propose a simple system that you can use to propel yourself and your kids forward in any area of life. We must focus on prevention in order to save our kids from years of future treatment.

Although this book is for parents, it's not really a parenting book. Parenting books deal with the way you act with your kids. They teach you to respond instead of react. That is important strategy and there are many quality books to teach you that skill. However, this book works from a different perspective. This book is about tapping into what is already there in your kids. It is about removing common barriers that hold your kids back.

This book fills a need for parents looking to optimize their children's potential. There are plenty of good books on children's health that focus on diet and lifestyle. However, these do not discuss how to employ your child's brain and mind for the best success. Likewise, there are many quality books on fostering children's emotional maturity and imagination. However, they skip over the importance of optimizing the physical brain as the foundation required to apply these principles. This book is a primer to provide your child with everything they need to maximize their own potential.

Think of it this way. If you put a NASCAR driver into an old jalopy and threw him out on the track could he compete? Of course not. You could put Dale Earnhardt, Jr., one of the best drivers in the world, into a Ford Edsel and he wouldn't stand a chance. This might sound ridiculous but I'm making the point that the vehicle is just as important as the driver. The driver is your child's mind and the vehicle is their brain and body.

You could be the best caring parent in the world and do all the right Dr. Phil type stuff. However, if you are not simultaneously optimizing your child's physical brain, their core equipment, then you are missing a key part of the formula. This book is about doing that.

What will you gain by reading this book?

In order to achieve any goal related to improving your life you need two things. The first is a reason with the desire to achieve the goal, and the second is the knowledge with an action plan to get it done. The pages in this book will provide you with both of these. Each chapter discusses a specific issue related to your family's success, with focus on the benefits of understanding the issues, and an ACTion™ plan to make the necessary changes.

I encourage you to read this book to identify the areas where you see the need to improve. Some of the content in these pages will set off a light bulb in your head for a 'eureka' moment. Other parts may simply reiterate things you already know. Yet other parts you might flat out disagree with. That's good. You should never read anything blindly. You must adopt philosophies that align with your own character and teach your kids to do the same.

In this book:

- You will gain a unique perspective and an ACTion™ plan that will help you raise successful children.
- You will learn how your child's physical health affects their brain, why you should be concerned and what you can do about it.
- You will learn the importance of downtime, relaxation and sleep for intellectual function.
- You will learn how to bring out your child's creativity and independence.
- You will learn how to create adaptable thinkers to prepare your kids for success in the inevitably fast-paced world they will face as adults.

The underlying philosophy in this book is that it is our job as parents to promote our children's success by giving them the tools they need to accomplish their dreams. Don't be a dream stealer. Don't hold them back. All kids have big ambitions in their heads. They don't need us to design a life for them. All they need is for us to help them break through the barriers that hold them back and get out of their way. They need us to cheer them on. They need us to support them physically, emotionally and socially. This book will help you identify the barriers that are holding your kids back and provide you with a plan to remove them.

Life is a challenge and perhaps one of the greatest challenges is doing a good job as a parent. Everyone comes to parenthood from a unique perspective. Some of us go into parenthood scared to death. Others go in overjoyed. Others go in believing that parenthood is their chance to undo all the stuff that their parents did to them. Yet in the end, it never turns out quite how we expected.

We all know that kids don't always do what we want them to do or react to situations the way we think they will. That's a good thing. It means they are individuals and march to their own beat.

Who should read this book?

This book is for parents who want their kids to achieve their maximum potential in life. It might sound like this book is for all parents. What parents would not want that? However, there is a subtle distinction in the first sentence that I want to make very clear. This book will help parents draw out their child's unique potential. It is not for parents that want to impose their own vision of super stardom onto their children. This book is for parents who recognize their child as a unique individual and is not for parents who are guiding their children to fulfill the dreams that they, as parents, were unable to reach. If you are a parent who recognizes your child's individuality and want to help maximize their success then read on. If you already have your child's life mapped out for them then put this book down. It is not for you.

CHAPTER 1
SET IT UP—FEEDING DREAMS

I believe that kids have a birthright to lead successful lives. As parents, we simply need to feed their dreams by providing them with the necessary tools. Feeding dreams means to nourish your child's brain and body with good eating, exercise and sleep habits, to nourish your child's mind through learning experiences and to nourish their spirit through reflection and self-development.

There is a law of physics that says 'a body in motion will stay in motion until acted upon by a force to stop it or change it's course'. I believe that kids are born in motion and on a course for success until someone acts on them to change their course. Buckminster Fuller, the engineering genius of the mid-1900s had this to say:

> *"All children are born geniuses. 9,999 out of 10,000 are swiftly, inadvertently, degeniusized by grown ups".*

Although this quote is somewhat whimsical, it is more insightful than first appears. I spend a great deal of time in Chapter 7 discussing the beliefs that we arm our kids with. This quote is more accurate than you might think.

Another law of physics says 'a body at rest will stay at rest until acted upon by a force to move it'. So many kids are inadvertently stagnated and halted along the pathway to growing up. Many will stay stagnated for much or all of their adult lives. We must act as a force to move them and keep them in motion.

Biology has programmed us all to develop and grow up. This is unpreventable. Our children will grow up. We simply need to supply them with tools that they need to stay on a trajectory for success as they do. Sometimes this requires our action to help them. However, sometimes it requires our inaction to allow them to find these tools themselves. Sometimes we just need to get out of their way.

The unfortunate reality of today is that most kids are not getting what they need to grow up to their potential. The trends of modern society have erected barriers that hold our kids back. This is not by design. I am not a conspiracy theorist suggesting some grand plot. It's just an unfortunate reality. The nutritional value of our foods have declined, physical activity is no longer a daily routine, hectic schedules prevent appropriate rest and sleep, formulaic teaching methods are stripping creativity, the freedom to dream is squashed by the need for financial security. These are all common barriers that prevent most kids from reaching their true potential. It is our job as parents to take proactive measures to remove these barriers from our kid's lives or empower them to break through the barriers themselves.

Feeding the mind, body and spirit

This book has two main sections. Each section is comprised of several chapters that focus on different major areas that children need to become their best. I suggest that you read them in order because each chapter builds from the one before.

It is like building a house. Before you can start construction, you must level the ground and dig out for the foundation. Then you pour the foundation, let it set and start framing the walls. Then the roof goes up and the exterior walls are covered. Finally, you work on the interior and apply the finishing touches. If you don't follow this sequence, the structure might look good for a while but it will not be sound and risks falling apart.

The beginning part of this book is like leveling the ground. It conveys an attitude about physical health that you must adopt. If you don't believe in the cause, you will not succeed in the mission. You must understand why physical health is so important in your children before you can start applying the foundational principles to achieve it. Next, you can build a strong framework of independence that will stand all tests of weather. This allows the addition of the finishing touches that bring out imagination and creativity. Your child will become a person of sound body and sound character that will contribute great things to his or her world.

Laying the Foundation of Physical Health

Giving your kids the gift of physical health is crucial for them to maximize their success. I will outline the importance of nutrition, physical activity and adequate rest in creating optimal health today and for the rest of their lives.

If you already try to feed your children well and ensure that they get enough physical activity and downtime then I applaud your efforts. I will reinforce the importance of these efforts and explain why they are so critical for your children's life-long success. You will understand how physical health actually 'rewires' the brain for success. You will understand how the value of physical health goes far beyond physical fitness and weight control and actually optimizes the mind, brain and body.

If you are currently less than proactive about your child's nutrition and physical activity, I hope to give you the motivation you need. I will explain why ignoring this important issue is like letting your kids play on the freeway in heavy traffic. The studies are clear. Unhealthy youth grow up to have a much greater chance of getting seriously ill as adults. If you choose not to acknowledge this fact you are setting your kids up for a life of ill health. This might sound harsh, but it is an undeniable truth.

Building Creativity and Independence

We must also foster creativity, imagination and independence. In order for kids to succeed in life, they must think clearly and act with confidence. You will learn how a physically healthy brain is a much better scaffold to build creativity and leadership. In the second section of this book I talk about how the process of acquiring these traits, through new experiences, actually feeds back to improve brain function. Amazingly, the interaction between physical health and intellectual experience cooperate to strengthen brain circuits that control stress and emotion.

There is ample scientific evidence that a physically healthy lifestyle contributes substantially to mental health. The foods you eat, the amount of physical exercise and sleep you get, definitely influence your mood, your confidence, and your level of independence.

The degradation of either physical or mental health can create a downward spiral in both of them. It is our job as parents to promote the upward spiraling in our kids. We must ensure that when they have left our nests to pursue their own independence that they have momentum in the upward direction. They will face many challenges in early independence. Their physical and emotional health and the strength of their own beliefs in maintaining them, will largely determine their response to these challenges. We must arm them now with empowering beliefs and habits. The focus of this book is about how we can do this by addressing each of these in a systematic plan to feed their dreams and their potential.

I would be remiss to cover the topics that I do without providing you with a plan to improve. Each chapter ends with the systematic ACTion™ approach to identifying the areas in which you need help, giving you a clear plan of what to do and monitoring your progress. So many books jump straight into doling out advice without first determining whether you need it.

Have you ever had a telemarketer call you at home and jump straight into a breathless 2-minute sales pitch before they take the time to determine if you might need their product? We all have. Why do they do that? If they just asked a couple of questions first to determine your interest, they could save themselves so much time. Then they only need to make their recommendations to the right people.

For example, I live in a 6-year old house. It's in good condition because it's fairly new. However, on several occasions I have answered the phone to find telemarketers selling windows. They go through the sales pitch without breathing and ask if they can come out and do an estimate. I finally get the chance to tell them I live in a new house and don't need windows. They quickly drop the pressure when they realize I am not a good prospect. If they would have found out that information first, they could have saved both of us a lot of time, made more calls and captured more sales.

The ACTion™ plan that you will find at the end of each chapter will revisit that chapter and help you evaluate your personal needs. It will help you hone in on the areas that you need the most help, so that you can efficiently move forward with improving your family's life and not try to fix things that aren't broken. Most people can use at least some help in each of the topics that I discuss, but you might find that you have some of them under control. That's great. We need to find that out up front so that we don't waste your time. As a parent, I know you are busy, so let's get you what you need and move on.

The ACTion™ system will take you through three basic steps, specifically designed for each topic area. The general steps are:

1. **A**ssess your situation and evaluate your strengths and weaknesses.
2. **C**ommit to taking action to fix the holes identified in the first step.
3. **T**rack your progress, provide feedback and adjust the plan if necessary.

I will take you through a detailed analysis of each chapter topic using this system. You can identify the areas where you need work and the areas that you are already doing well. To make the most out of the ACTion™ plan at the end of each chapter get the Action Guide at http://www.thebraincode.com/ActionGuide.

Let's get started right now and jump into laying the foundations for your child's physical health.

SECTION 1

LAYING THE FOUNDATION OF PHYSICAL HEALTH

CHAPTER 2
GET IT IN—NUTRITION

In this chapter, you will learn how your child will benefit now and in the future by understanding some simple concepts about nutrition. You will understand how feeding your child well now will propel them to achieve their potential later. I discuss the benefits of making good nutritional choices and the short- and long-term consequences of ignoring the issue.

You will also get a simple plan that you can use to ensure your child's health today and for the rest of their lives. You won't have to track calories or spend hours with food calculator to track all the nutritional information that some experts want you to do. A couple of basic concepts with your own common sense go a long way.

Although the theme of this book is building the best brain you can in your kids, much of this chapter focuses on nutrition that is good for the body as well. Many brain researchers like to think that the brain is somehow separate from the body. I don't.

The brain does have its own protective mechanisms and needs that I will discuss at the end of the chapter. But realize while you're reading, what's good for the body is good for the brain.

The War within Your Child's Body

There is a war raging within our bodies every day. On the one side are environmental toxins that we breathe, drink and eat and on the other side are our body's defense mechanisms that fight to keep us healthy. This is not new. There are 'natural toxins' all over our environment. Things like disease causing germs, radon gas and other natural contaminants that get into our food, water and the air we breathe. This battle has been going on for thousands of years.

However, environmental toxins have dramatically increased over the past century providing an increased threat. Our body's defense systems just don't adapt at the same rate. It is also problematic that the foods we eat have declined in nutritional quality. This puts us and our kids at greater risk since our bodies require this nutrition for ammunition against the environmental threats.

Casualty Report

When we think about things like hardening of the arteries (atherosclerosis) and adult-onset diabetes (type II diabetes), we don't typically think of these as childhood illnesses. However, children are diagnosed with chronic illness more and more all the time. Some would argue that this is simply due to an improvement in early diagnosis techniques. While this is certainly a factor, it is undeniable that the rate of many chronic diseases is increasing in children and adults alike.

A large national study called the PDAY study (predeterminants of atherosclerosis in youth) actually showed that 1 in 5 high school age kids today already have the beginning stages of atherosclerosis and the majority of youth have fatty streaks in their arteries. They may not feel them yet, but they are there, looming over their future. The Center for Disease Control predicts that 1 out of 3 kids born after the year 2000 (1 out of 2 for some minorities) will develop diabetes due to current nutritional trends in the United States. This is an alarming trend for parents who don't want to see their kids get sick; and an alarming trend for a nation that can't handle the increasing burden of health care for its citizens. We can do something to change this.

We must reverse these trends. Kids are not immune to chronic disease caused by poor lifestyle choices. I hear all the time "they're just kids; they can handle it". This is absolutely false. Lack of quality nutrition in our kids is allowing the slow accumulation of damage to mount up in their veins and organs until one day it hits a point where they are diagnosed with a preventable disease.

Chronic illnesses that will catch up to them in adulthood are not the only problems. There are many immediate threats as well. Poor nutrition is associated with attention deficit hyperactivity disorder (ADHD), asthma, eczema and behavioral problems. This is not to say that poor nutrition is the sole cause of all of these disorders but it can definitely contribute. In many cases, improved diet and quality nutritional supplementation can reverse or at least improve several childhood disorders and help prevent chronic illness in adulthood.

Oxidative Stress Threatens Your Children's Future
One of the major on-going battles is the body's attempt to keep damage from oxidative stress at a minimum. Many experts now believe that damage due to oxidative stress underlies the cause of several chronic degenerative diseases. There are certainly other factors at work, like genetics, but oxidative stress appears to be a significant player.

What is oxidative stress? It's a simple concept really. Oxygen is a double-edged sword. We absolutely need it to survive but it's also what ends up killing us in the end. Without it, we cannot produce the high-energy demands of our physiology. However, the highly reactive properties of oxygen that make it so useful also make it very dangerous.

We mostly use oxygen in a reaction to convert foods we eat into a molecule we use for energy, called ATP. However, the process of using oxygen to make ATP actually releases very damaging molecules called free radicals. These little suckers can rip through your cells and create tons of havoc, damaging all kinds of things including your DNA. This process is called 'oxidative stress' and if left unchecked can contribute to the development of all kinds of disease like cancer, multiple sclerosis, Alzheimer's dementia, Parkinson's disease and many more.

The damage caused by oxidative stress slowly accumulates until it is bad enough to cause disease. It really just depends on where the greatest damage happens that determines the type of disease. For example, oxidative damage in the eye can lead to macular degeneration; in the joints to arthritis; in the arteries to atherosclerosis. That is where genetics comes in. Oxidative stress will be more likely to get a foothold wherever you are genetically weakest. But the underlying molecular mechanisms of these varied diseases can have a similar root cause—too much oxidative stress.

Anti-Oxidants to Your Child's Rescue

Luckily, our bodies have ways to deal with oxidative stress. We have genes that have the specific job of 'capturing' free radicals before they wreak too much havoc, minimizing the damage. This defense mechanism is sometimes called our anti-oxidant system.

Many vitamins and plant-derived nutrients, like vitamin C and vitamin E also act as 'anti-oxidants' and are required by our bodies innate anti-oxidant systems to keep free radicals under control. This is why it is so incredibly important to get enough of these nutrients into our bodies because without them the damage from oxidative stress accumulates over time until it causes major health problems. The body's own systems are not sufficient. We must arm it with anti-oxidant molecules from our diet and supplements to optimize our defenses.

Your Child's Enemies

Unfortunately many 'kids' foods' are not providing them with the needed protection and some are actually increasing oxidative stress. To make matters worse manufacturers of unhealthy foods are spending a huge amount of money to get your kids to eat their offerings. The fast food industry spends about $11 billion per year promoting their products while the US government only spends about $350 million promoting healthy living. This is an outspending of 30:1 in favor of unhealthy foods. Our kids don't have a chance against this marketing machine. This is one reason you might not be fully aware of the issue. The marketing campaigns do a masterful job at hiding the truth.

These same companies also have a hold on our schools. Vending companies offering unhealthy products litter the hallways of schools all over the country. Companies are capitalizing on the financial woes of our schools by making them offers they should refuse. Most schools that allow vending machines are actually getting a kickback of all sales. This makes it in the schools financial interest to promote the sale of these health degrading items and, in fact, they are doing just that. Many of the schools that offer processed food snacks also allow the manufacturers to operate advertising campaigns within school property. I strongly encourage you to ask about your school's policy when it comes to allowing vending machines in their hallways.

There are, however, good people on our kids' side. Ann Cooper is a 'renegade lunch lady' who helps school districts around the country revamp their school nutrition programs. She is very proactive in helping kids get the nutrition that they need. You can go to http://www.thebraincode.com/offers to access an exclusive interview with Ann where she describes her efforts and what parents can do to help. You can also get her new book 'Lunch Lessons: Changing the Way We Feed our Children'.

To the credit of some fast and processed food companies, they are showing a willingness to improve. Several fast food restaurants now offer juice or milk instead of soda and fruit or salad instead of fries. Also, the major soft drink companies have willingly replaced soda in school vending machines with their own brands of bottled water. This is certainly a step in the right direction. Still, most of the items on fast food menus or in school vending machines are far from healthy, yet these are the ones promoted in campaigns.

Kid's Meals are a Bad Idea

The whole concept of 'kid's meals' or 'kid's foods' is insane. The idea behind kid's meals started several decades ago because kids don't eat as much as adults. The food service industry supplied a smaller portion size at a reduced cost to serve this need. However, kid's meals have since evolved into lower quality, high sugar, high fat foods with minimal nutritional value. This promotes the philosophy that it's okay for kid's to eat differently than adults. Again, this is insane.

It's true that kids have not developed the taste for rich foods and don't like many of the things that adults eat. But this is no excuse to feed them garbage. There are plenty of healthy foods that kids enjoy—you just have to identify them. Studies tell us that we should keep offering kids vegetables and other healthy foods, even if they don't like them. Eventually they will develop a taste for richer foods and develop healthy eating habits.

If you continue to allow your kids to eat 'kid's meals' simply because they protest a little bit then you are robbing them of developing tastes for diverse foods that will lead to healthy eating habits as an adult. You might say "But my kids don't like anything good for them". I guarantee that you can find healthy foods that your kids like.

I realize that this is a huge problem for parents of fussy eaters. However, every time we give in and let them eat the unhealthy foods that they like we are making it worse. If things are out of control for you, seek the help of a child nutritionist. You children's lives are literally at stake.

Chef Ann has a great analogy for this. She compares kids complaining about eating vegetables to complaining about schoolwork. If a child comes home from elementary school and says 'I don't like math, I'm not going to take it anymore', we don't just say 'OK, we'll find something else that you do like'. No, children must learn math and learn to read because they are kids and that's what's good for them. We must approach nutrition in the same way. They must get appropriate nutrition because that's what's good for them.

Keep the Bad Guys Behind Bars

I could go into an extensive list of all the bad foods that our kids eat but I think most parents have the common sense to know what these are. I will highlight a few of the major offenders and the reasons why you should minimize these in your child's diet. I am not going to be an extremist and suggest that you should never allow your kids to eat these foods. They are part of the American experience. They are the foods you find at the ballpark, at BBQ's and at birthday parties. You can't feel guilty every time your kids eat these foods because it's not practical to avoid them all of the time.

However, many kids eat these foods as a staple part of their diet. This is when it becomes a huge problem. These foods are creating oxidative damage as I discussed above and the body's anti-oxidant systems cannot handle all of it. To make matters worse, the kids who eat these foods on a regular basis are also the kids who are not getting adequate anti-oxidant protection from multiple daily servings of fruits and vegetables.

It's all about risk. Every time you allow your kids to eat poorly you do a little damage and every time you encourage your kids to eat well you add a little protection to deal with or reverse the damage. If you continually tip the scales in favor of the damage, your kids are going to have a high probability of health problems.

French fries are one of the biggest offenders today because they are fried in oils containing a large amount of trans fats. Even many of the frozen fries that you buy at the supermarket to bake at home are already coated with trans fat. The national academy of sciences has recommended that the acceptable daily level of trans fat in the diet is zero. That's right; you should not allow your kids to eat ANY trans fats. They oxidize easily to produce free radicals that I discussed above. They will damage your kids' arteries and predispose them to a life of chronic heart disease and other problems. Unfortunately, the majority of school age children get most of their 'vegetables' in the form of french fries. You should minimize all fried foods in your own and your kids' diet.

Hot dogs and other highly processed meat products are also major offenders. They have large doses of compounds known as AGEs, which stands for advanced glycation end products. These form in the manufacturing process when using high temperatures to cook foods with high protein or fat content. Without going into all the biochemical details, they do exactly what their name implies. They damage your cells and make them age faster, partially due to increasing oxidative stress. Studies are emerging that show AGEs are a major bad guy in our diets. If you haven't heard of them already, you will. Unfortunately, this is not something that has made it onto food packaging labels yet. Just don't let your kids eat too many hot dogs or other processed meats.

Other kid's staples like cheeseburgers and pizza are not great choices either. They also have a lot of AGEs because of the way they are cooked. But additionally, most fast-food burgers do not use lean meat so they have a very high saturated fat content. This goes for the meats on pizza as well. In addition, cheese is very high in saturated fat and you should not allow excessive amounts in your child's diet. Personally, I love cheese but I have cut way back because of the high levels of saturated fat. It's just not worth it.

The bottom line is to minimize saturated and trans fats found in red meat, dairy and fried foods and to minimize AGEs found in processed or over-cooked meats. The closer you stay to fresh, unprocessed foods, the better off you will be. Most people are already aware of this but I hope that I have given you a little extra motivation to follow through. I believe that if you can visualize the consequences going on inside your and your child's body after eating these foods, it will be easier to avoid them. Again, it's about risk. The more you allow your children to eat these foods the more you increase their risk of health problems down the road.

This is also where genetics comes into play. People that have a family history of specific chronic diseases can fall victim to them much faster if they increase their risk through poor dietary choices. Other's may have a strong genetic constitution and can handle a little more. However, NOBODY is immune to the damage of a poor diet. We all play by the same biological rules. Some people just have a little better equipment. If you have no illness in the older members of your family don't think you are off the hook. The foods you put into your kids' mouths will help define who they become.

A Word about Trans Fats

Trans fats should absolutely be avoided in yours and your children's diets. A couple of decades ago we thought these were 'healthy' alternatives to saturated fat and used them to make margarines and all kinds of other products. Now we know that they are horrible and you should avoid them completely. The FDA recently made it mandatory to list trans fats as a category on food labels. Check for them and avoid them. Also, check the label for 'partially hydrogenated oils'. If you see this ingredient, put it back and find a similar product without it. The process of 'partially hydrogenating' creates trans fats. Even if the label shows zero trans fats, they are there. The FDA does not require foods to list trans fats when they are less than 0.5g but they should be avoided even in these small amounts.

Your Child's Allies

Quality nutrition is not rocket science. Don't be overwhelmed by all of the latest studies you hear in the media. These are usually sensationalized anyway. Common sense goes a long way in creating a healthy eating plan for your family. You don't need to worry about all the complexities of what is the perfect meal plan for your kids or understand all the physiology. You just have to understand a few simple principles and act with them in mind.

When talking about quality nutrition you can boil it down to two things: micronutrients (vitamins, minerals, etc.) and macronutrients (protein, carbohydrates, fats and fiber). You can go a long way to ensure quality macronutrients by cutting out things that you already know are unhealthy and replacing them with better choices, like the suggestions below.

Carbohydrates and Fiber for Efficiency

Fiber-based carbohydrates are important to create and maintain health. Fiber is required for optimal performance of your child's digestive system and helps their bodies absorb the nutrients from other foods. Carbohydrates are the source of energy that our bodies use for fuel. Please don't subscribe to the 'low-carb' fad diets. They are a shortsighted approach to weight control and I don't recommend them. You can get fiber and quality carbohydrates from two major sources.

First, fruits and vegetables come to the rescue again. These have high fiber content along with all the other good stuff they contain. Second, use whole grain products as much as possible in breads, pastas and cereals. Stay away from foods with refined flour as a main ingredient. The refining process removes much of the quality fiber (and vitamins). Just check the labels for 'whole' grains to get quality fiber and carbohydrates.

It's important to understand that plain 'wheat' bread is not the same as 'whole wheat' bread. Only the whole wheat (or other whole grain) bread has the entire unrefined grain that you need. Also, breads and cereals that are 'fortified with vitamins and minerals' are usually a joke. The refining process strips out a couple dozen vitamins and minerals, puts eight or so of them back and calls it 'fortified'. Stick with those that have whole grains as the first ingredient.

Protein for Power

Proteins are another component of the diet. Proteins contain the amino acid building blocks that will keep your child's body strong. There are many high quality protein sources from plants and meats. The main concern with getting most or your protein from red meat is to keep the saturated fats to a minimum. Chicken, fish and eggs are much lower in saturated fat than beef. Plant products that have high protein include nuts, quinoa (keen—wah), soy and several kinds of legumes. Again, variety is the key. Most Americans are not deficient in protein. In fact, the opposite is usually true.

Fats for Fluidity

The final major macronutrient is fat. Yes, you need fat. Fat is the main component of membranes that surround every cell in your body. In fact, brain cells have so much membrane around them that the brain is about 60% fat! Don't subscribe to all the 'low fat' diet plans either. Fat is a required component of a healthy diet. The important thing you need to do is to distinguish between 'good fat' and 'bad fat'.

Mono- and poly-unsaturated fats are good for you (in reasonable portions) and necessary for your kid's health. They are required for normal development and are incredibly important for maintenance of your child's cardiovascular system, immune system, brain and eyes. Olive oil is a good source of monounsaturated fat and fish oil is a great source of polyunsaturated fats, which include omega-3 fats that are so important in our diet. The labels of all food products will show total fat and break that down into saturated fat and trans fat. Use this information to minimize these bad fats and you will be going a long way. Some labels may go further and list the mono- and polyunsaturated fats as well but this is not currently required.

Arm Your Children with Antioxidants

Fruits and vegetables are the major source of antioxidants in our diet. This is why it is so important to consume several portions of a variety of fruits and veggies every day. Without them, you are leaving your antioxidant system unarmed and allowing free radical damage to accumulate. A good rule of thumb is to eat 3–4 different colored fruits and veggies every day. The color of the fruit actually represents the type of protective anti-oxidants that the fruit/veggie has. By eating red, yellow, green, orange, purple, etc. fruits and vegetables, you are ensuring a variety of anti-oxidant protection that will help you adapt to many types of oxidative attack.

Supplement for Full Protection

A great diet including varied anti-oxidant protection, fiber, protein and good fat is crucial to maintain day-to-day health, but studies show that it is not likely to be enough for optimal disease prevention. Supplementation with a good multivitamin is also beneficial for your child's long-term health. Studies show that multi-vitamin supplementation probably lowers the risk of chronic diseases like cancer, diabetes, Alzheimer's, depression and many more. In fact, a large study published in the Journal of the American Medical Association in 2002 strongly endorsed the use of multi-vitamins in disease protection.

Why do we need supplements? Our ancestors never took them. This is true, but there are many differences between today and yesteryear. First, a much smaller number of people lived to a ripe old age than today so they didn't worry as much about diseases of old age. Second, the quality of nutrients from food was higher than it is today. A study published in the American Journal of Clinical Nutrition in 1999 shows the degradation in our diet over man's history. This study highlights how vitamin and mineral content of our foods has declined while saturated and trans fat quantities have increased. Third, the oxidative stress causing agents were much lower in our environment than they are today. If you subscribe to the 'I can get everything I need from my diet' mentality, you are missing a huge opportunity for protection. Most experts now support supplementation with vitamins and minerals. However, be clear, they are 'supplements' not 'substitutes' and can not replace a quality diet.

Choosing an Appropriate Supplement

With all of the 'health products' and multi-vitamin/multi-mineral products on the market, how do you choose? You should know a couple of things to help clarify your decision. Many nutritional products on the market are not of high quality for a few main reasons. Either they are low-potency, sub-optimal formulation or manufactured from poor ingredients.

First, let's look at potency. When looking at the label on the back of a bottle of vitamins, forget about the RDA (Recommended Daily Allowance). The RDA was developed in the 1920's as a recommended dose of daily vitamins and minerals to prevent malnutrition. This is very different from the amount needed for optimal health and prevention of chronic disease. When people say 'you can get everything you need from your diet' that is true if you are talking about the RDA and preventing malnutrition. It is not true for most people if you are talking about optimal health. A one-a-day multi-vitamin that has 100% RDA for everything, right down the line, is not likely sufficient.

Second, you should pay attention to formulation. This is the total amount of each vitamin and mineral and the ratios in which they are present. Some vitamins can be taken in high doses and provide strong anti-oxidant protection, like vitamin C and vitamin E. Other vitamins should not be taken in high doses because they can actually become toxic in large amounts, like vitamin A. Minerals like calcium, magnesium, and iron, etc., must also be taken in controlled amounts. This is why it is imperative to find a quality nutritional company. You need to know that they have done the research and developed a well-formulated product. I have some suggestions following the next paragraph.

Third, the FDA regulates the nutritional industry in the 'food' category. This means that nutritional products are required to meet the same standards as ice cream, hot-dogs and frozen waffles. This is not very encouraging news for people looking for a quality product. The quality and cost of raw materials that nutritional companies purchase to manufacture their products vary greatly. This is why there is a huge discrepancy in prices of the final products. Cheap ingredients lead to cheap final products. A few companies self-impose the FDA's regulations for the pharmaceutical industry. These companies produce nutritional products at a much higher standard. You may have heard the term 'nutraceutical' or 'pharmaceutical grade' nutrition products to describe these. If companies follow these guidelines, they can put the 'USP' symbol on their labels, which stands for United States Pharmacopia and ensures a higher quality product.

However, don't confuse quality with potency. Companies might use pharmaceutical grade manufacturing practices and put USP on the label but still provide a very low potency formulation. You need both—high quality ingredients and formulations.

A great resource for learning more about how vitamins work and comparing the quality of most North American brands is a book by Lyle McWilliam called, 'The Comparative Guide to Nutritional Supplements'. There is also a version of this book for kid's products called 'The Comparative Guide to Children's Nutritionals'. For information on specific high quality nutrition products that I recommend, you can visit http://www.thebraincode.com/supplements.

Strategizing to Win the War on Disease

What if you could train your brain to crave healthy food? Wouldn't it be nice to give up the cravings for sugar and sweet stuff and get to a healthy lifestyle without really trying? The brain knows what the body needs. A complex system of hormones monitors the gut and bloodstream and alerts the brain to what is needed. The problem is that most people's diets are so out of whack that the brain loses control over what's good for you and goes into 'addiction' mode to crave what feels good at the time. You can adopt a way of eating that gives your brain back the control it needs to help you crave healthy choices.

First, you have to care. You have to take the knowledge that you have learned in the above sections and assimilate it. You have to understand that if you choose to ignore nutrition you are dramatically increasing the chance of chronic disease in you and your children. In fact, if you are not convinced, I advise you to stop reading this section right now and start the chapter over. Read the first section again and understand what the consequences are for ignoring your kid's nutrition. Picture them as adults. Are they overweight in their 20's and 30's? Are they having chest pains in their 40's? Are they on medication to lower their cholesterol in their 50's? The action you take right now definitely has an impact on the answers to these questions. We don't typically think about our kids in their later years but your actions today will indeed help define who they will be as mature adults.

The Glycemic Index is your Key

Let's start with how you can adopt healthy eating habits without fighting the cravings all the time. Have you ever experienced that energy crash and craving for sweets in the middle of the day? It frequently happens a couple of hours after eating lunch. I know you have. We all have. What is that and how can we avoid it for our kids and ourselves? It all relates to the glycemic index of foods, which is just a measure of how fast they burn in our body.

A high glycemic food, one that has a lot of sugar or simple carbohydrates, will burn very fast and cause your blood sugar to rise very quickly. This gives you an instant energy pick-me up but the problem is that it doesn't last long. The body needs to maintain blood sugar in a very tight range. Therefore, when your body senses your blood sugar rising quickly from a high glycemic meal it will release a high dose of insulin and that forces your blood sugar back down. I will go into more detail about specific high and low glycemic foods a bit later.

The problem with high glycemic meals is that they force your body to 'over react' in order to get your blood sugar back down and this causes your blood sugar to crash very quickly. This has two bad effects. First, it makes you feel very tired. Second, since your blood sugar actually falls below normal, it makes you crave a sweet snack to get it back up again.

This sets off a vicious cycle of raising and crashing your blood sugar, which messes up your energy levels during the day and causes you to over-eat sweet, simple-carbohydrate rich foods. This often leads to weight problems. See the picture below that illustrates this.

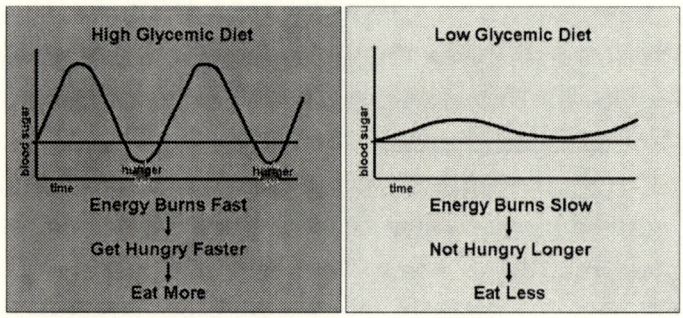

However, there is also something much worse than weight gain going on. Eating high glycemic meals causes the body to go into high gear producing ATP because of all the sugar in the blood. This drives free radical production up as well and increases oxidative damage. If high glycemic meals are the norm in your kids diet then high oxidative damage is the norm as well. A 2006 study published in the *American Journal of Clinical Nutrition* evaluated markers of oxidative stress in the blood after different meals. This study found a strong correlation between the glycemic index of the meal and the level of oxidative stress markers detected after the meal.

Furthermore, the body can eventually adjust itself to stop crashing the blood sugar by becoming resistant to its own insulin. After this happens, the stage is set for diabetes and all the health problems that go along with it.

This downward spiral is such a simple thing to prevent. Simply replace high glycemic foods with low glycemic foods that burn much slower. You will stabilize your kids energy, help them develop habits that will lead to good weight control and dramatically lower any risks of diabetes and other chronic diseases.

This practice is so amazing you will not believe how well it works until you do it. Once I started eating low glycemic foods, I completely lost the craving to eat sweet stuff. Not only that but I just don't get hungry as often. When you switch to low glycemic meals your body will naturally reset itself to your appropriate weight without even trying to lose pounds!

What foods are we talking about? A good rule of thumb is to avoid white foods like white bread, white rice and potatoes. These are high in simple carbohydrates that burn much too quickly. Replace these with whole grain alternatives and many fruit and veggie choices. If this would represent a huge change for your kids' eating habits then that is even more reason that you have to do it. Kids are more freaked out by the idea of 'whole grain' than by the taste. There are so many varieties of healthy whole grain products, I'm sure you can find something that everyone enjoys. Next time you are at the store take a few extra minutes to look at the labels. Try to avoid products with flour as a main ingredient and find those that have whole grain instead.

For example, replace high-sugar breakfast foods such as sweet cereals, donuts, pastries and syrup-soaked pancakes, with high fiber, whole grain choices. There are many great tasting whole grain cereals and breads. It's easier than you might think and your metabolism will thank you immediately. It is also wise to get some protein into the breakfast meal. Protein does not contribute to the glycemic index because it does not raise your blood sugar. Getting some protein at breakfast will give your kids increased and sustainable energy throughout the day and help them perform better in everything they do.

Another telltale sign of a high glycemic index food is 'high fructose corn syrup' in the ingredients. You will find this in soda pop and many other 'kids drinks'. Replace them with 100% fruit juices or even better, water. Keep in mind that too much fruit juice isn't good either. If you or your kids drink a can or more of soda on a daily basis, simply removing this from your diets will have a huge effect on your energy and weight.

You also need to realize that it is not about weight control. If you or your kids need to lose weight it will happen naturally through a low glycemic diet, but that is not the reason to do it. Even if you do not have a weight problem, you should start eating primarily low glycemic foods.

They will keep you healthier in the long run and give you the sustained energy you need to keep alert throughout the day.

The Glycemic Load

I want to touch briefly upon a slightly more complex concept, the glycemic load. As I already discussed, the glycemic index is a measure of how fast a food burns. The glycemic load is a measure of how much of a 'sugar-spiking punch' that the food has.

You should understand this subtle distinction. There are some foods, especially some fruits, that have a relatively high glycemic index but they are still good for you because they have a low glycemic load. For example, bananas are high glycemic and burn very quickly. This is what makes them great foods for athletes during sporting events. They provide a quick burst of energy that you sometimes need. Yet, they have a low glycemic load. They don't spike your blood sugar very high so your body does not need to over-react with a high dose of insulin release. This is in contrast to a candy bar, which will also give you a quick energy burst but will spike and crash your blood sugar as I described.

The glycemic load is really a combination of the glycemic index and the total calorie content from carbohydrates. Foods can burn quickly but only pack a few calories, like bananas. These are fine. Foods that burn quickly and pack many calories, like white bread have a high glycemic load and you should avoid them.

Teaching your kids to snack on low glycemic foods and offering mostly low glycemic foods at mealtime will set them up for a lifetime of healthy eating habits. How cool is that? Actually wanting to eat healthy and enjoying it!

Eat Small and Often

Another eating habit that is beneficial to long-term weight control and good health is to eat often. That's right, don't wait until you're starving and gorge down a huge meal. Eat small meals often. For your kids, this means you should keep healthy snacks like, fruit, nuts, trail-mix and low glycemic energy bars at arms reach. Let them graze between meals as long as they are grazing on healthy, low glycemic foods.

Also, when it comes to mealtime get in the habit of using smaller plates. If you always eat off a large 10-inch dinner plate then you want to fill it. There is no reason for this. Eating off smaller 6-inch plates encourages smaller portions, which are quite adequate, especially if you have allowed healthy grazing between meals.

When my parents were growing up in England during World War II, meals were rationed. They grew up with the philosophy that you should eat everything on your plate because there wasn't much to eat. Food wasting was simply not allowed in our house. After all, there are starving kids in Africa! How many of us heard that growing up? I never understood how I could help the African kids by eating everything on my plate.

Minimizing food waste is a great message. However, eating more to waste less is not the right way to do it. Smaller portion sizes that can be easily finished are the right way to go. Please don't force your kids to eat everything on their plate. If they always have food left over, then give them less and encourage them to take less when they control their own portion size.

In my field of scientific research, I have the opportunity to interact with people from all over the world. The one thing that always surprises non-Americans is the huge portion sizes that are the norm in our country. It's simply not necessary to eat as much as we do. One of the major problems is that we allow ourselves to get too hungry between meals. Eat smaller meals more frequently and graze on healthy foods when you're hungry and you will go a long way towards minimizing the total amount of food you eat.

Another critical habit is to eat breakfast. Studies show that when kids eat a good quality breakfast, that burns slow and maintains steady blood sugar levels, they perform much better in school. Breakfast also sets the nutritional stage for the rest of the day. A good low glycemic, whole grain breakfast with fruit, will set your energy levels and reduce your cravings for sweet foods throughout the day.

Once you get started with a low glycemic diet your body will reset itself and stop craving sweet foods. Once you're there you can start to trust your instincts. Your body knows when it needs protein, carbohydrates or fats. The brain is an incredibly sophisticated machine and actually senses what nutrients are low and sends out signals to eat foods that contain those nutrients. However, you have to be operating optimally to be able to trust these signals. A low glycemic diet will get you there.

Hydrate

Of course, adequate hydration is critical for your child's health as well. You must ensure that your kids drink plenty of good, clean water every single day. Most people do not drink enough water and live their lives in a constant state of dehydration. I'm not talking about life threatening dehydration (at least in the short term), but sub-optimal hydration. It's estimated that about 75% of Americans continually experience low-grade dehydration. This causes fatigue, headaches, muscles aches, and a general feeling of blah.

Many kids and adults alike get much of their daily fluids from soda or sweetened drinks. Drinking plenty of water every day will make you less hungry and lead to lower calorie intake. It will also give you more energy and allow your brain to think more clearly.

Some people say that they don't like water. This is learned. Water is necessary for life and we have been drinking it for millions of years. People that don't like water have simply replaced their thirsty desires with other addictive beverages. Break this cycle and get back to drinking water. This alone will make a huge difference in the way you and your kids feel on a daily basis.

Bringing it Back to the Brain

Let's get back to the brain. This book is about optimizing brain potential. A brain that is running like a 'well-oiled' machine is a big part of that. What's good for the body is good for the brain. Removing the barrier of poor nutrition will allow the brain to function optimally as well. This is the first step in maximizing potential.

The Brain is an Energy Hog

However, the brain does have specific needs that go beyond the rest of the body. First, the energy demands of the brain are huge. About 10% of the energy you eat goes to support the brain, even though it only accounts for about 2% of your body weight. Remember our discussion about ATP production. Well, there is a huge amount going on in the brain and the potential for free radical generation is equally high. The brain requires a lot of anti-oxidant protection. This is another reason to eat a lot of those fruits and veggies and take quality vitamin supplements. They provide nutrients that are especially good for minimizing free radical damage during ATP synthesis. Eating lots of fruits and veggies help protect against diseases like Alzheimer's and Parkinson's for this reason.

The Brain Needs Good Fat

Another differentiation for the brain is the fact that it is about 60% fat. The brain is one big fat organ. One of the crucial nutrients that the brain needs is a special kind of fat, called omega-3 fats. These are incredibly important for both brain and body function. They are essential fats, meaning your body can't make them and must get them from the diet or supplements. The major source of brain friendly omega-3's comes from fish or fish oil supplements.

Of course, one concern about eating too much fish is the mercury and heavy metal contamination. Please take care in buying fish oil supplements because of this. Many manufacturers do not adequately remove these from the oil before packaging them for sale. You should look for fish oil supplements that specifically state they have been 'molecularly distilled' to remove contamination. To learn about specific supplements that are free of mercury and other heavy metals visit http://www.thebraincode.com/supplements.

Another class of fats required for brain function is the omega-6s, which also must be obtained from the diet. The balance between these two types of fat is extremely important because they compete with each other for many physiological processes. We obtained about a 1:1 ratio of these fats through most of man's history and this is the optimal ratio. Unfortunately, today's western diet contains about a 30:1 ratio, in favor of omega-6s. This is because omega-6s are found in high concentrations of many foods we eat today, especially corn oil. Although, most people are getting plenty of omega-6s, they are comparatively deficient in omega-3s.

This can lead to huge problems for the brain. Studies suggest that a deficiency in omega-3s leads to increased rates of suicide and violent behavior. This is probably because low omega-3s in the diet are thought to decrease the availability of brain chemicals called dopamine and serotonin. Low brain dopamine is associated with depression and low serotonin is associated with schizophrenia and psychotic behavior.

The relationship between decreased dietary omega-3s and these mental health conditions is currently a hot topic of study. In fact, this is the current focus of my own research. This is a prime example of how nutrition can have a direct effect on brain function and behavior. However, this is only one example of thousands. What you eat dramatically affects the way you feel.

If you are interested more on this topic, I have interviewed Dr. Alan C. Logan, the author of a great book called 'The Brain Diet'. Dr. Logan is on the faculty of the Harvard Medical School's Mind-Body Institute and in this interview, he talks about how to eat for optimal brain function. An audio recording is available through http://www.thebraincode.com/offers.

Nutrition—Recap

We covered many detailed concepts in this chapter. If you feel that you need to read it again then please do so. Here is a quick recap of the main points.

- Oxidative stress can lead to many chronic diseases.
- Anti-oxidants from supplements, fruits and vegetables protect against oxidative stress.
- Kids and adults need a good balance of fiber-based carbohydrates, protein and healthy fats.
- The glycemic index is important for energy balance and weight control.
- The brain requires a lot of energy and a lot of anti-oxidant protection.

ACTion™ Plan

Now that you are armed with compelling reasons to attend to your child's nutrition and have some idea about how to do that, let's solidify the plan and hold yourself accountable to take action. To get the most out of the ACTion™ plan and move your children's lives forward you can download the companion Action Guide at http://www.thebraincode.com/ActionGuide.

The Action Guide will take you through the 3 steps below in a plan for success.

1. **A**ssess your own eating habits and evaluate where you need help.
    - Honestly evaluate your current situation based on what you learned in this chapter.

- Are you and your kids getting enough of the right kinds of foods and supplements?

2. Commit to action and begin to nourish your family well.
    - Take out the trash. Throw away the junk food. You don't need it and it is holding you back.
    - Plan your meals to ensure that you get ample servings of fruits and veggies, fiber-based carbohydrates, lean protein, healthy fats and enough vitamins and minerals.
    - Make a grocery list based on your planned meals and get the right foods into your household.

3. Track your progress and celebrate success.
    - Repeat the assessment in step 1. How are you doing with your plan? Do you need to make any realistic modifications to get back or stay on track?
    - Don't forget to celebrate your success!

The next chapter will help you build on the foundations you are laying

CHAPTER 3
WORK IT OUT—PHYSICAL ACTIVITY

Everyone knows that exercise is good for them. It contributes to *weight loss* and weight management. It's good for your heart and your cardiovascular system and it generally keeps you fit and healthier.

However, did you know that exercise is also good for your brain? It can actually improve brain performance. Not only that, but exercise can help prevent brain disorders like *Alzheimer's disease, Parkinson's disease* and *depression*. It even increases your chances of recovering from a stroke or traumatic brain injury.

In this chapter I discuss why keeping your child physically active is critical. You will learn simple things that you can do today, using exercise to help your children handle the pressures of school, social situations and other potentially stressful environments. You will also learn how exercise contributes to brain health and how exercise protects your child against brain disorders in their later years.

State of the Union

It shouldn't surprise you that kids today are more sedentary than any generation before them. The availability of video games and hundreds of TV channels in the average American home has redefined the way that kids play today.

Unfortunately, this trend, coupled with nutritional problems discussed in the previous chapter, has led to astounding increases in childhood obesity. Between 1965 and 2002 the average body weight of elementary school children rose by 10 pounds! It is even worse in teenagers. Today about one in five American kids are considered overweight.

The 2006 government survey, the 'National Indicators of Well Being', found these statistics: In 1980, 6% of school age children were overweight; by 1994 this figure rose to 11%; by 2000, 15% and the latest data from 2004 finds that 18% of school age children are now overweight. How long will we allow these statistics to climb? How many kids will we put at risk of serious health problems before we stop! See the graph on the following page that illustrates the problem. Think forward five, ten or fifteen years. Where will we be when your kids are having kids? It is up to us, as parents, to reverse this trend now.

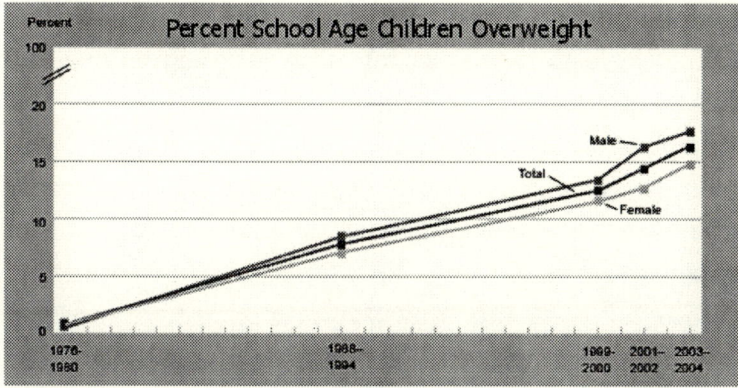

Source: http://www.childstats.gov/amchildren06/hea.asp

Kids that are more physically active have far lower rates of obesity, which should be no surprise. But it's not only about obesity because this is just the predecessor to so many illnesses, including diabetes, heart disease, kidney failure, cancer, etc. Childhood obesity is not just a cosmetic problem. It is setting kids up for a lifetime of chronic pain and medication. It seems like a new study comes out every week linking obesity to another chronic disease. I know you don't want this for your children.

Even if your kids do not have a problem, our society does and we are all part of that. The economic toll that the obesity epidemic is having on our health care system is immense.

Whose Fault is it?

Kids today have much greater restrictions on their freedom. They can't usually roam the neighborhood like many of us used to do. They can't just take off on their bikes, ride across town to their friend's house and find something active to do. We just don't allow them to leave our sight as much anymore due to safety concerns in today's world.

When I was a kid, I could call up half-a-dozen friends after school and organize a pick-up soccer game at the local school or get a rousing game of capture the flag going. Today parents just don't feel comfortable letting their younger kids take off for a few hours to go and entertain themselves. This requires a little more creativity on our part to keep them active.

Are Organized Sports Right for Your Children?

Today most kids get a lot of their physical activity through organized sports. This is a great option for some kids but others just don't fit into this structure as well or just don't like playing sports for any number of reasons. Some kids are pushed too hard or alienated too young if they don't perform to expectations. Others just don't enjoy competition. If your kids don't enjoy sports, it is still important to keep them active. I'll get into that more in a minute.

If your children do enjoy organized sports then this is a great option. However, I encourage you not to get too specialized in a single sport at a young age but to participate in multiple sports throughout the year. If you limit kids to one or two sports, you may be preventing them from finding their niche. They may excel in an area that you don't expect. I believe that kids should not really specialize (for most sports) until they reach their early teen years, at least.

Furthermore, athletic diversity will provide multiple experiences for the brain and body. By engaging in different activities, they will develop a diverse set of muscle groups and fine motor skills. This also increases the development of different pathways in the brain that I talk more about in Chapter 5. For more information on youth athlete development and the importance of diversity listen to an interview with Brian Grasso at http://www.thebraincode.com/offers. Brian is an expert on developing youth athletes. He has worked with kids, Olympians and professionals all around the world.

If, however, organized sports are not the answer for your kids then you must find a physical activity that they enjoy and can do on a regular basis. It doesn't have to be complicated. Just playing outside is good enough. It's impossible to suggest activities that will work for everyone because of varying environments, time schedules, physical abilities, etc. The important thing is to ensure that your kids do something to get their heart rate elevated on a regular basis.

How Much is Enough?

We used to think that kids should get about one hour per day of physical activity. However, new studies show that in order to maximize the prevention of disease markers for heart problems (and probably other problems as well) later in life, kids need more.

A study published in *The Lancet* in July 2006 shows that kids around 9 years old should get about two hours per day and kids around 12 years old should get about 90 minutes per day of physical activity. Again, this does not need to be an organized activity. Riding bikes, climbing trees, running or just playing at the playground, all add up.

Perhaps this is not a problem for you because your kids are already very active. Great. Keep that going. If this is difficult for you then you must make it a priority and actually schedule time into your kids' day when they must do something to get them breathing heavy. Limiting TV and video game use is a must that I will discuss later.

One question that many parents of active children ask is, 'how much is too much?' I talk about the importance of down time in the next chapter.

Schools and Over-Protective Parents are not Helping

Unfortunately, we can't rely on the schools to exercise our kids anymore because physical education is being cut from many curriculums. Some schools cite budget concerns while others have liability fears. In fact, some schools are even disallowing games that involve running on recess! If this isn't the most insane thing I have ever heard, I don't know what is. At the time of this writing, some school districts across at least half a dozen states have implemented policies to control recess activities. Some schools have outlawed standard games like tag, soccer and kickball, to name a few.

School officials are so worried about legal action for kids that fall down and get hurt that they are promoting unhealthy living. Kids get hurt! This is part of life and it's an essential part of growing up. Over-protective parents that do everything they can to prevent skinned knees and elbows are not doing their kids any good. It seems like every time anyone gets hurt in our society today we look for someone to blame.

When my oldest son was in 1st grade, he came home one day with a chipped tooth. It turns out that a teacher opened a door into a hallway and hit him as he was walking by. The school wasn't very upfront about the fact that a teacher was responsible. I'm sure they were concerned about liability. We could have raised a big stink and got into the whole issue, but we didn't. Kids get hurt. It was an accident and that was that.

Where is the Voice of Reason?

Parents must unite against the trend of decreased physical activity in school. Whether these decisions are for liability or budget reasons, it makes no difference. It is not doing our children any good. If we don't step up to protect our kids' health from this bureaucracy then who will? Don't assume that the local governments are looking out for your kids' interest on this topic. They may not be.

For more information on the importance of physical activity, listen to an interview with Dr. Dean Miller at http://www.thebraincode.com/offers. Dr. Miller has played and coached professional sports, trained NASA astronauts and hosted a national television show about fitness. He now talks to middle and high school kids about physical education and life goal setting.

Sweat to Protect Your Kids

Hundreds of studies show the protective effects of moderate exercise. Regular exercise lowers rates of so many diseases that I can't list them all. This is why it is so important to establish a habit of physical activity in our kids. Exercise is the closest thing to a fountain of youth that we have been able to find.

Set the Example

The first thing that we, as parents, need to do is to role model. We can't expect our kids to follow the 'do as I say, not as I do' rule. It just doesn't work. You must adopt the behaviors yourself that you are trying to instill in your kids. My kids see me get up and exercise almost every morning before I do anything else. This will have a lasting impression on their attitudes about physical health when they reach independence.

The amount of exercise an adult needs is not as great as that of our children. So, you don't have to get out there and run around with your 9 year old for two hours a day. The optimal amount of physical activity for adults is under debate, but on the low end, you should get 20–30 minutes of exercise, 3–5 days per week. Most studies show that about 30 minutes every day is optimal. Of course, you should always check with a prevention-minded physician before starting any exercise routine. If you haven't exercised in years then be realistic about what you can do to start, but don't think that you can't do it. It all starts with a few simple steps.

To get the most out of an exercise routine you should be getting your heart rate up to about 80% of your maximum, defined as 220 minus your age. I am 40 years old at the writing of this book, so 220 - 40 = 180 and then 80% of 180 = 144. This means I should get my heart rate up to about 144 beats per minute for 30 minutes every day to get the optimal benefit from exercise.

Although you can use chest straps or hand grips to monitor your heart rate, I have always been a proponent of just listening to your body. Unless you are training for a competitive event, you don't need fancy equipment to measure your heart rate. You can simply hold your wrist or neck to count the beats over one minute to determine where you are.

Once you get a 'feeling' for the level of exertion that this corresponds to you can simply listen to what your body is telling you. You should feel like you are breathing heavy but not so out of breath that you can't talk. You should be sweating but not feel like you are overheating. The more you do it, the better you get at listening to your body. However, if defined routines work best for you then do that.

Don't try to force yourself to participate in an exercise plan that you don't enjoy. It will not work. I'm sure there is something physically active that you enjoy doing. Playing tennis, running, swimming, briskly walking, riding your bike or wrestling around on the living room floor with your kids are all great options. What did you like as a kid? Take off the work suit, put on some workout clothes and just do it!

Breaking into the Habit

Many of us were active and healthy in high school but then just seemed to let it slip as we enter our adult years. Life gets busy, our metabolism slows down so that we can't get away with eating as we used to and things get out of control.

A good friend of mine found himself in this position about ten years ago. He drank too much soda, ate poorly and found himself suddenly 50 pounds overweight about 15 years out of high school. He decided he'd had enough and told his wife "I'm going for a jog." Although he was very active in college, he had been inactive for so long that he couldn't jog far and had to walk much of the 1 mile effort, but he kept at it. He stopped drinking soda continued to exercise and lost 15 pounds in a month. He started to ramp things up slowly and participated in 5K and then 10K runs. He had caught the bug to keep going.

His brother and sister-in-law had run marathons and tried to convince him that he should try one. He painstakingly got himself up to a 10-mile run, figured that a 26.2 mile marathon was "impossible" and couldn't be done. Ten years after the day that he took those first steps, he had completed nine marathons and countless smaller runs. He lost 50 lbs and found himself in the best shape of his life at the age of 42. It all literally began with a few simple steps.

Build a Buffer

Studies also show that exercise specifically protects the brain from aging and injury. Older adults that regularly exercise perform better in cognitive tasks and have lower rates of Alzheimer's and Parkinson's disease. They also recover stronger from strokes and from accidental brain injury.

One can argue that people who exercise have many factors in their lives that can contribute to lowering disease risk. For example, they smoke less, eat better, etc. However, studies in laboratory animals confirm that exercise itself is protective. Animals that are exercised are protected against traumatic brain injury in laboratory tests and don't develop the extent of Alzheimer's and Parkinson's disease in model systems. Exercise is the best medication you can take. This is one prescription that you can feel great about dosing up your kids with.

I know that we don't often think of our kids as mature adults, but that is where they are heading. The behaviors and values that you promote today will have a life-long effect that can help protect them for many years to come. Use your foresight today to ensure a long and healthy life for your children.

Studies show that people tend to continue their lifestyles choices from an early age. Ignoring the value of physical activity now will make them more likely to do so as adults. In order for our kids to be cognitively active adults all the way through life, we must instill the importance of physical activity today. If we do not, we are doing them a huge disfavor.

Treat Yourself to a Good Workout

In addition to exercise's protective role, it is a valuable treatment tool for existing diseases of the brain and body. Fitness training improves cognitive functions relative to planning, scheduling, task coordination and attention. Adults who exercise have more grey matter in the brain, than adults that don't exercise. This essentially means that they probably have increased brainpower. Exercise also effectively treats depression and other mood disorders.

Outside of the brain, exercise has a plethora of benefits as well. In adults, exercise improves diabetics' ability to regulate their blood sugar and maintain their weight. It helps people improve their cholesterol levels by decreasing the 'bad' LDL—and increasing the 'good' HDL-cholesterol. It improves the recovery rate and the remission rate in some cancer patients by boosting immune function. Again, the benefits are endless.

A Workout a Day...

Physicians have been touting the benefits of exercise for years. Now we are beginning to understand why it is so good for you. Exercise actually causes hormonal changes in the brain and body that help regulate hunger to keep you from overeating, improve the immune system's ability to fight disease and improve clarity of thinking.

Do you remember the anti-oxidants that I talked about in the chapter on nutrition? I told you that our bodies have their own natural anti-oxidant systems. We have genes that have the job of capturing free radicals generated during the production of energy. Well it turns out that moderate exercise actually turns on these genes responsible for activating our anti-oxidant system. This is likely to be a major reason underlying many of the known benefits of exercise. By activating the body's anti-oxidant system exercise actually promotes the repair of damage caused by oxidative stress.

As I said in the first chapter, oxygen is a double-edged sword. It is necessary for energy production to keep us alive but it is also the source of many toxic free radicals generated during that production. So, it would seem that exercise, which causes deep breathing would actually create oxidative stress. In fact, many experts in the past thought that might be true. However, studies have discovered that exercise actually cranks up the anti-oxidant protection system so that this oxidative damage from moderate exercise doesn't happen. The body figured out how to get all the benefits of exercise and prevent the consequences! The innate wisdom of our bodies never ceases to amaze me.

Activate your Mood
In addition to all these physical benefits of exercise, there are mental benefits as well. This is another reason that physical activity is so important for maximizing your child's potential.

It turns out that physical activity actually turns on hormonal support systems in your brain. Exercise causes a rise in several growth factors in the brain that are responsible for helping brain cells survive and divide into new brain cells, or neurons. As far as we know, only a couple of brain regions can produce new neurons in a mature brain. Exercise increases the amount and rate of neuron production in these regions. The hippocampus is one of the main brain regions for new neuron birth and is very responsive to physical activity. Exercise actually increases neuron birth in the hippocampus and causes it to grow. Why is this important?

A major role for the hippocampus is in the response to stress. In fact, many studies show that people with stress disorders, like post-traumatic stress disorder, have a smaller hippocampus. Too much stress can actually damage the hippocampus and cause neurons to die, the opposite of what happens when you exercise. Exercise increases the size of your hippocampus and studies show that this can protect you against stress.

Folks that have taken up exercising regularly know that they are much more capable of handling stress throughout their day than they were before they started exercising. This is probably, in part, because exercise and stress have opposite effects on the hippocampus and exercise improves your 'buffer' to handle the stress.

Interestingly, anti-depressants work in a similar way. Although, we don't completely understand exactly how anti-depressants work, we do know that several classes of anti-depressants increase new neurons in the hippocampus. They do the same thing that exercise does! They both activate growth factor systems in the brain that cause new neurons to grow in the hippocampus. Psychiatrists have known for a long time that most patients experiencing depression respond much better to therapy if they combine it with regular exercise. In some cases, exercise alone is even sufficient to alleviate depressive symptoms.

With so many kids and adults on anti-depressants today, I have to wonder what proportion of them could get off these medications with more physical activity. Of course, anti-depressant therapy is both beneficial and necessary for some folks. However, the rate of prescriptions today, especially in kids, is out of control. In many cases, we turn to the 'quick fix' of drugs before addressing the possible causes of the problems—which in many cases are lifestyle choices.

Activate Attention

Another major role for the hippocampus is that it plays a critical role in learning, memory and attention. Exercise improves cognitive function and the ability to focus. A consistent exercise routine or just consistent physical activity combined with good nutrition can actually improve your child's performance in school and lead to *better grades*.

A large Canadian study looked at the academic performance of kids split into two groups. One group received one hour of PE (physical education) class with moderate physical activity during the course of the day, while the other group had academic instruction for that hour. At the end of the year, the group of kids that had PE outperformed the other group in academic subjects. This was true even though the non-PE group received about 15% more classroom instruction. So does it make sense to cut PE from our schools? Absolutely not!

Physical activity increases attention, improves learning and improves memory. These are all attributes that help kids become better students. Yet our schools continue to cut PE from their curriculums, citing the budget. We, as a society, must put greater value on physical activity in the school system and find a way to support it.

Wiring the Brain for Success

Exercise literally rewires the brain. Exercise increases the number of connections between brain cells, which has the effect of creating new circuits. So exercise rewires the brain to optimize the ability to process new thoughts and respond to stressful situations.

Additionally, exercise increases the number of blood vessels that supply several brain regions. This has the effect of improving nutrient delivery and waste removal from critical regions that effect mental function. So not only does exercise help promote new brain circuits, but it also promotes feeding and maintaining brain circuits as well.

In chapter 5, I will get into more detail on how creating new pathways and circuits in the brain are beneficial for your children. For now, just remember that physical activity promotes brain circuit growth while sedentary behavior promotes brain circuit shrinkage. Which one do you want your own kids to experience?

Creating Momentum

If you or your kids aren't currently getting daily physical activity, getting started can be the hardest part. Remember, don't try to do something that you won't enjoy and don't try to jump into an unrealistic training plan all at once. If you currently are not exercising at all then saying that you are going to get up early every day and work out for 30 minutes is not realistic. There are some simple things that you can start doing right away. Then you can gradually increase until you reach an optimal program that you are happy with.

To get your kids and yourself more active you need to replace sedentary times with active times. Right? One simple way is to limit TV and video game time. In our house, we call it 'screen time'. This is anytime the kids are either watching TV or playing video games or just surfing on-line. Our kids get a set amount of screen time each day. The only thing that is an exception to screen time is actually doing homework or productive projects on the computer.

The American Academy of Pediatrics recommends limiting screen time in school age children to no more than 1–2 hours per day of non-violent, educational programs. However, on average, kids are watching about 4 hours of non-educational TV per day. This amount of TV exposes your kids to about 20,000 commercials annually (mostly promoting unhealthy eating) and an average of 8,000 murders by the time they leave grade school.

One rule that works for some people is to have your kids 'buy' screen time with physical activity. You can have your kids 'bank' time by playing outside or being physically active. For example, 1 hour of physical activity buys 15 minutes of screen time. My concern with this method is that it turns physical activity into a chore or something they have to do to get what they want. The goal is to make physical activity fun. Still, if you like the idea you can try it and see how it works.

Be a Role Model

The ideal way to promote physical activity in your entire family is to find things that you can do together. Brainstorm a list of physical activities that you enjoy or that you would like to try. Involve all family members in the process. If you live in an area where the seasons change dramatically then these types of activities may be much easier in nice weather. Still I'm sure you can think of a hundred things to do.

In the summer you can go to the lake and swim, ride your bikes around town, go for walks after dinner, play tennis at the city park, shoot hoops in your driveway, play Frisbee in the park. There are so many things you can do. In the winter you can go sledding, go skiing, go ice-skating, build a snowman in the backyard, make a snow fort and have a snowball fight.

Most kids are happy to get out and do stuff like this, especially if you do it with them. As adults we get so busy with 'adult stuff' that we often forget how much fun little activities like these can be. If necessary, you can just schedule them in a couple of times per week. This will boost your biology with all of the advantages described in this chapter and bring your family closer together at the same time. It's a win-win.

Get Addicted

Once you find physical activities that you enjoy you will get addicted. I guarantee it. You will feel the need to get exercise and you won't feel as good if you don't get it. This is a great addiction to have. It's not that you will feel worse when you don't exercise than you felt before you started. It's just that exercising will make you feel so much better. If you fall out of your routine, you will feel like you did before you started exercising, and you won't like it.

If you exercise on a regular basis, you know exactly what I'm talking about. If you don't exercise now, imagine this. Think of how you feel on a daily basis. I'm sure that some days are better than others are. Imagine feeling great most of the time. Imagine that your current good days actually become your normal days and your new good days are so much better. This is what exercise will do for you. You will be amazed.

Working Out—Recap

I hope I have given you sufficient reasons to promote physical activity in your own kids. Let's do a quick recap.

- Exercise prevents chronic diseases of the brain and body.
- Exercise treats many diseases that you might already have.
- Exercise improves brain function including memory and attention.
- Exercise helps you handle stress.

ACTion™ Plan

Now let's get into the specifics of what you can do right away. For best results, download the Action Guide plan from http://www.thebraincode.com/ActionGuide. We'll go through the ACTion™ system designed to get the most out of this chapter.

1. **A**ssess how much physical activity you and your kids are getting.
    - How much daily exercise are your kids getting? Is it enough?
    - How much weekly exercise are you getting? Is it enough?
    - Be honest with yourself.

2. Commit to improving your kids physical health and start the process.

    - Brainstorm a list of physical activities for you and your kids for all weather conditions. Be sure to consider your financial budget in this process

    - Schedule times to do these activities and write them onto your calendar. Be sure to include some when you will exercise as a family.

    - Tell a couple of friends what you are doing, so that you make a contract with yourself to follow through on your plan. This is an incredibly important step in order to keep you moving forward.

3. Track your progress and reward your success.

    - After 1 month, repeat step 1 to see if you are getting enough exercise.

    - Make any necessary modifications to ensure you have a realistic plan.

    - Don't forget to celebrate your success!

The next chapter will help you balance all of this activity with the necessary downtime that you and your kids need.

CHAPTER 4
SLOW IT DOWN—SLEEP AND RELAXATION

In this chapter, I discuss the importance of downtime. I talk about downtime in the form of rest and quiet time as well as in the form of sleep.

In today's society the temptation is to keep our kids busy all the time. My wife and I have been guilty of that ourselves. However, it is so important to build downtime into our children's schedules. It is necessary for healthy development of the body and the mind. Too much structure can actually impede creative thinking. I will finish that thought in chapter 6.

The perfect balance between activity and inactivity will vary from child to child. You, as the parent are the best one to judge what is right for your child. However, understand that downtime is critical. For some kids it's going to be more important to promote activity because they will naturally gravitate towards downtime. Others may actually need you to promote downtime because they are always moving and never want to take a break. You need to find the right balance. This chapter will help you do that.

Downtime is necessary for your child's physical, mental and emotional development. They need time to let their bodies recover and their minds go quiet. Everyone needs time to sit quietly and go into their own thoughts in order to become independent people. Some people never really learn to be comfortable by themselves. They don't like to be alone because they don't know how to occupy their time with reflection. They have a tendency to rely too much on input from the outside world. I will discuss the importance of both physical and mental rest in its different forms.

Rest for Physical Development

Every great athlete understands the importance of rest as part of a training program. This chapter is not about breeding athletes but the same principles apply to normal development.

A body builder trying to develop muscle will not work out the same muscle groups every day. They understand that the workout actually breaks their muscles down so that they can be built back up a little stronger. Resting muscles is a key part of building them. This is true for kids as well.

A long distance runner will not train all the way up to the day before an event. They understand that muscles need to rest for a good long time before they are called upon to perform. A marathon runner may train hard for months leading up to a race but will typically cut their routine back the week before the actual event.

When I was training for a marathon, I actually refused to run for even 2 days in a row. I knew that my body needed long rests between training runs. This is not typical. Many runners will go 5 or 6 days a week and only take off one day for rest. However, I knew that my body did not perform well that way so I only ran 3–4 days per week in my marathon training. Required downtime varies widely with each individual.

Likewise, parents need to pay close attention to the level of exertion their kids are putting out. Some kids might be able to handle a lot of physical activity with no sign of fatigue while others obviously struggle and need more rest. In either case, downtime is critical and you must be the judge for your own children.

I have always been opposed to high intensity daily practices for school sports. I think it is crazy that kids are required to work out every day and compete in high level games with very few breaks in the week. By the end of the typical school sports season, the players are broken down and in serious need of recovery time. Their schedules put them at greater risk for injury, which is not helping them or their team. Not to mention the potential negative affect on their academic performance as well.

My father coached high school soccer for many years and understood this principle. However, he met resistance when he tried to implement more rest into the season. He approached the athletic director in the high school where he coached with his concerns about the physical health of his players. He felt that the daily practice routine pushed his players too hard and wanted to give them one or two days a week of rest. The response that he received was "No, you can't do that." He was told that they had to be out there every day. He was able to adjust his practice intensities to provide them with the break but the underlying attitude persists in school sports today.

I truly believe that if we implemented more downtime in our school sports we would see a vast improvement in the athlete's performance come game time. They would have greater strength and energy. But so many coaches are dogmatic about 'more is better.' It's simply not true. These kids are not professional athletes and their bodies should not be called upon to act as if they are. Downtime is critical.

Visualize the Alternative

Visualization is a great technique to give athletes the much-needed downtime and continue to develop their abilities. Top Olympic athletes and professionals use visualization. When I was playing soccer in college, we had regular meetings with our sports psychologist to learn visualization techniques.

Visualization is a great supplement to practice and has the added bonus of resting muscles. The technique works by having a player visualize in their own mind, a successful scenario repeatedly. For example, a soccer player might visualize shooting on goal. They would see themselves stepping up to the ball with perfect balance and striking it with perfect technique. They would see the ball driven into the goal by placing it precisely in the corner.

The technique works because it activates some of the same brain circuits as if the player were actually striking the ball! This strengthens those circuits so that they operate more efficiently during the real event. I talk about strengthening brain circuits in chapter 5 and discuss how it optimizes brain efficiency.

I have used sports as an analogy but the technique works for other scenarios as well, like learning to play a musical instrument, learning to dance or learning lines in a play. The key is to visualize perfect action in order to strengthen the circuits responsible for perfect results. The concept that practice makes permanent holds true. Only perfect practice makes perfect.

Downtime for the Mind

Equally important as downtime for the body, is the downtime for the mind. As I said earlier, it is important to teach your kids how to be alone and comfortable with their own thoughts. If kids are continually busy with sports, school activities, music lessons, dance classes, etc. then they never really get the opportunity to reflect and develop their own unique perspectives. The longer they go without learning this life skill, the harder it is to learn it later.

Many people don't even realize that they lack this skill until later in life, if at all. It is never too late to develop but it is a lot easier to develop at a younger age. Being alone is very different from being lonely. Everyone needs alone time, even if you have a very supportive network of intimate relationships around you.

If you have difficulty with this yourself, there is an entire industry of 'relaxation' techniques available. Different things work for different people. I am simply trying to convey the importance of finding something that works for you and your children. This is such an easy skill to ignore. Busy kids and adults alike have little time to sit quietly and relax. However, it is as important as anything else in maximizing your child's and your own potential.

There are many common and easy to do habits to help your kids, depending on their age. For kids that are old enough to write, journaling is a great way to promote this skill. If you keep a journal yourself then you already understand the value of this. If not, you should consider starting one and do the same for your kids.

You can simply write down what you did that day or be more reflective about creative ideas or feelings that you experienced. Ninety five percent of the good ideas that we have are lost because we don't record them. Journaling is one approach to recapturing some of these. I highly encourage you to promote journaling in your kids at a young age. Not only will this help develop reflection skills and increase awareness of self-worth, but also it will be an invaluable document for you later in life. The great business philosopher, Jim Rohn, says, "A life worth living is a life worth recording."

For pre-readers, simply playing alone with some toys that stimulate imagination is great. Kid's have incredible imaginations. Keep them going. Toys or games that require kids to interact and create worlds in their own minds give them the basis to build strong independence later on. There is no need to be caught up in the perfectly designed toy unless you are trying to develop very specific skills. Just use common sense and promote imagination. For example, figurines that involve role-playing or building block toys that involve creating drive kids to use their imaginations.

Of course, there are higher end relaxation techniques like yoga, meditation, etc. To be honest, I don't know much about these but they are definitely something that I have on my own list of things to learn. There is so much value in deep relaxation that most people never explore.

Sleep on It

The ultimate form of downtime is sleep. We obviously need to ensure that our kids get enough sleep. We all need to sleep. As much as I would like to have more hours in the day, robbing them from my sleep time never seems to work. There are physiological reasons for this.

Yes, some people need less sleep than others and you need different amounts of sleep at different points in your life. For kids, sleep is incredibly important for their mental and physical development.

Biological Rhythm

We have an innate 24-hour rhythm built into our bodies and our brains. A huge number of hormones go up and down during the course of the day. This is called our circadian rhythm.

The brain sets a 'clock' for release of specific neurochemicals at specific time points. In fact, we have a set of genes known as our 'clock genes'. The activity of these genes is primarily set by daylight. This is the brain's own way of monitoring day and night and knowing when it should be sleeping and when it should be awake. People who don't get enough sleep can disturb this system and that can lead to mood and cognitive problems.

A specific part of the brain, called the hypothalamus, is mostly responsible for keeping track of the body's circadian rhythm. This part of the brain controls many other body functions as well, including the immune system, reproduction, hunger, thirst, and body temperature. This means that sleep and the control of many other body functions are tightly coupled, so disturbing your sleep cycle can have consequences for these systems as well.

Another important hormone that sleep regulates is growth hormone. This hormone plays a major role in stimulating growth of muscles and bones and is primarily released during sleeping hours. A lack of sleep can lead to a lack of growth hormone release and affect the development of muscles and bones.

This is a potential problem in middle and high school children. The school schedules that are common in the United States are completely out of sync with what we know about physiology. High School kids need a lot of hormonal support to maintain their rapid rate of development through puberty and adolescence. Sleep is required to enable this hormonal support and the extremely early hours that we force these kids to get up are not healthy.

Without revamping our school system, the only thing we can do as parents is to get our kids to bed early so they get the good night's rest that they need. Kids in middle and high school have a social tendency to be night owls. You must resist allowing this for their own good. If we rob them of critical sleep, we risk disturbing hormonal systems required for optimal development.

Recharge the Batteries

Sleep is literally a time for the brain to recharge. Just like a rechargeable battery is 'filled up' again by putting it on the charger, so does sleep recharge our brains. Activity during the day actually uses up brain molecules required for signaling and processing thoughts. This is one reason you feel like you can't think clearly when you get too tired. These molecules are re-made during sleep to fill the reservoir back up again for use the next day.

Studies show that growth hormones in the brain are at lower levels after sleep deprivation. These hormones are responsible for allowing the brain to create new connections during learning and they help maintain the connections already there. Sleep regenerates the brain, allowing enhanced performance the following day.

File the Memories

In addition to sleep effecting how you perform the next day, sleep also effects how well you learned the previous day. Huh? How can a good night of sleep affect what you learned the day before? Sleep is the time that memories are consolidated and strengthened. Even though your kids may get a good night's sleep before school, they will retain what they learn in school if they get another good night's sleep after school.

Research shows that the brain actually replays activities of the day during sleep and that this replaying strengthens the ability to recall the experience. This applies to both academic and physical experiences. Meaning that sleep helps consolidate 'muscle memory' from motor skills practiced that day or academic skills learned in class. Whether it is playing sports, playing a musical instrument, or reading, writing and arithmetic, sleep enhances the skill.

In a related study, researchers took two groups of people, taught them an identical task, and tested them on it three days later. One group was sleep deprived the night after they learned the task and the other group was not. Both groups got adequate sleep for two more nights so that neither was sleep deprived on the day of testing. The group that did not get enough sleep the night after they learned the task performed much worse on the test than the other group. This demonstrates again that consolidating experience the night after learning is just as important as getting adequate sleep before learning.

Sleep sets your kids up for a successful day by improving their attention and then it drives those experiences home by replaying them again.

Sleep Your Way to Better Grades

It should be no surprise that the quality of children's grades relates to the quantity of their sleep. Several studies have shown a strong correlation between performance in school and sleep schedule. Kids that get less sleep have worse grades. In some studies the difference in sleep is not that large between the 'A and B' students and the 'C and below' students. Some studies show that the average difference between these students is only about 30 minutes of total sleep time. This suggests that a little extra sleep goes a long way.

Another important factor that many parents may not have considered is the bedtime delay between school nights and weekends. Weekend delay of bedtime is a factor in school performance as well. Students that have greater than a two-hour difference between school night and weekend bedtime typically have worse grades than students who have a 1-hour delay or less. The shift in the sleep cycle can throw the circadian rhythm off and affect attention and learning. Also, as discussed earlier in this chapter, poor sleep on the weekends will impede consolidation of what was learned during the week.

Sleep for Mood

The interaction between sleep and brain chemistry applies for mood as well. There is an incredibly complex system of neurochemicals and hormones that regulate our mood. This has been a hot topic of research science for decades. We have made a lot of progress in understanding the system but are still really only scratching the surface. Sleep and the circadian rhythm have a huge effect on our mood. In some cases, lack of sleep can simply lead to irritability and lack of patience. In other cases, it can contribute to more serious mood disorders, like depression.

Every parent knows that when their kids don't get enough sleep they are cranky. Sometimes when they get too tired, they get down right nasty and unreasonable. We have all dealt with this. Well, there is a lot of neurochemistry going on behind the scenes in these cases. For one, lack of sleep disrupts brain serotonin levels, which play a major role in sleep and mood.

Total sleep is important and parents should ensure that their kids get to bed early enough to get sufficient sleep. The amount of time needed is variable from age to age and child to child but most parents have a feel for what their kids need. Typically, school age kids need more than 9 hours of sleep to perform optimally. Most kids need 9–10 hours per night.

Again, Studies have shown that kids with greater differences between their school night bed time and weekend bedtime have more daytime sleepiness, greater depressive moods and more sleep cycle problems. Typically, kids that have more than a 2-hour time difference between school night and weekend bed times have increased problems in these areas.

Sleep Off the Fat

Another major concern for children with insufficient sleep is obesity. People that sleep less have higher rates of obesity than those that get enough sleep. Several factors probably contribute to this finding. Sleep and obesity is not an obvious connection in most people's minds but the evidence is clear.

First, daytime sleepiness will be higher in those that get less sleep and that leads to lethargy and inactivity. This predisposes poor sleepers to get less physical activity and burn fewer calories than good sleepers. This is another great reason for a balance between activity and inactivity.

Second, the circadian rhythm also controls appetite. Getting less sleep can influence the hormone system that regulates when you are hungry. There are several neurochemicals in the brain that control when you feel hungry and when you feel full. The regulation of when they release into the bloodstream is partially controlled by the circadian rhythm. Studies show that poor sleep leads to increased hunger and overeating during the day.

Third, I told you earlier that growth hormone release occurs during sleep. Studies have found that growth hormone levels correlate with increased obesity. Growth hormone actually suppresses fat cell generation and increased fat suppresses growth hormone release. Lack of sleep facilitates this vicious cycle because sleep is when the body typically releases the most growth hormone. So if you don't get enough sleep and release enough growth hormone you can make more fat cells and gain more weight.

Establish Good Habits Early

Many adults live years in sleep deficiency. We must give adequate sleep a higher priority. I talked above about how the interaction between sleep and neurochemical systems runs deep. Sleep essentially affects everything we do. Unfortunately, our society is not designed to allow us adequate sleep. Work and school force kids and adults alike to get up early. Getting to bed early is not always easy either with our busy lives. If adequate sleep is a problem for your kids then you really need to take a hard look at everything they do and identify areas where they could slow down or cut back.

Bedtime Rituals

It is important to establish a bedtime routine for kids. This helps their minds associate things going on around them with that state of sleeping. I'm not saying you need to do a little song and dance or anything, just something consistent.

Brushing their teeth is an obvious one. Also, reading quietly in their room for a while is a great way to wind down. For the younger kids, a bedtime story is a great ritual for many reasons. It provides some bonding time, sets their mood for rest and increases imagination and creative thinking right before their minds go into consolidation mode.

Please don't let them watch TV in bed before going to sleep. First, I am a firm believer that kids should not even have a TV in their rooms. It gives them too much free access to a bad habit. Second, the stuff that goes into your brain right before you go to sleep gets a little extra processing, as I have been discussing. You don't want to put garbage into their minds right before bed.

You wouldn't tuck your kids into bed with that day's garbage, would you? Well, if you let your kids watch TV right before bed you essentially do the same thing to their minds. This is a bad habit that should go. I'm not saying that all TV shows are garbage, but you should be extra selective about exposure right before bed.

Adults should follow suit. Especially when it comes to watching the news in bed before you go to sleep. You are not doing yourself any good at all by filling your brain with stories about violence, war, rape and murder right before you go to sleep. In fact, you're not doing any good filling your brain with this at all.

I realize that your kids are not watching this type of show before bed (at least I hope not), but it is still a bad habit to get into. Children should not rely on television or radio to get them to sleep. They need to relax with nothing but their own thoughts. If you supply them with a crutch to get to sleep, it will be difficult to reverse later on.

In our home, we have 'bedroom' time that we implemented when our oldest child was about 3 years old. The kids spend about half an hour in their rooms quietly before lights out. They can spend this time reading, writing, drawing or playing quietly. This builds quiet time into every day and helps them go to sleep with a calm mind. We found this very effective at providing needed downtime.

Befriending the Sandman—Recap

The importance of sleep is not a new concept and it has immediate feedback when we don't get enough. We know when we're tired and it's easy to tell when our kids our tired, even though they rarely admit it. I hope this chapter has provided some insight into why adequate sleep is so important. I have tried to touch upon several different brain systems that sleep impacts so that you might understand just how screwed up you can get without sleep.

To recap, adequate sleep and rest are associated with the following aspects of your kids' lives.

- Rest is required for proper physical development and recovery for athletes.

- Downtime promotes reflection and the development of independence.
- Proper sleep is necessary to consolidate the lessons of the day and improves academic performance.
- Proper sleep is required for hormonal stimulation of muscles and bones.
- Proper sleep is required for normal function of the brain chemicals that control mood.
- Lack of sleep is associated with overeating and obesity.

ACTion™ Plan

Whether your kids need more sleep or just some more quiet time the plan below will help. The companion section in the Action Guide can help guide you through a specific plan for success with greater efficiency. You can download it at http://www.thebraincode.com/ActionGuide.

1. Assess your child's downtime and sleeping schedule.
   - Do your kids have a regular bedtime?
   - Do they get 9–10 hours of sleep and is that enough?
   - Do they have extreme delays in bedtime on the weekends?
   - Do they have any alone time to think quietly?

2. **C**ommit to ensuring they get enough rest and relaxation.
   - Look at your schedule and identify things that can go if your kids are too busy. Strike them off the schedule. Drop some activities if you need to.
   - Make sure that they have a regular bedtime and stick to it.
   - Don't let them shift from their bedtime by more than a couple of hours on the weekends.
   - Make sure that they get time to themselves. The half hour period before bed is ideal but if other times work better for you then ensure your kids get that time.
3. **T**rack you progress to ensure your plan is working and celebrate your success.
   - Repeat the step 1 assessment. Are you sticking to your plan? Do you need to make modifications so that you can stick to it?
   - How are your kids' attitudes? How is their energy level? How is their clarity of thinking?
   - Don't let a good job go unnoticed. Reward your success!

If you have taken action on the first section of this book then you are well on your way to maximizing your children's potential. The next section will help you build independent and creative thinkers using the optimized brains that you have given them.

SECTION 2

BUILDING INDEPENDENCE AND CREATIVITY

CHAPTER 5
SOAK IT UP—LEARNING EXPERIENCES

"Experience allows you to see potential. Inexperience forces you to see danger."
—Denis Waitley, Speaker and U.S. Olympic Team Sports Psychologist.

A variety of experience is so important for raising successful children. The above quote really hits the mark on this point. Experience allows your kids to approach situations with a variety of viewpoints. They will be able to find potential and opportunity where others with less experience might only see risk and obstacles. They will be able to act more quickly and decisively from a point of confidence when faced with tough choices. Experience actually creates physical changes in the brain that enable these capabilities that I will discuss in this chapter.

We must get our kids as much experience as possible. Of course, I'm not talking about formal work experience. I'm talking about life experience. Enjoying and seeking out new experiences is an incredibly important life skill. The world is always changing and life-long learning is imperative to excel in today's environment.

This chapter will focus on the importance of balance between challenging our kids with new experiences and allowing them comfortable routines. This is important for early childhood, to get the most out of critical periods of brain development. It is also important for later childhood, adolescence and even adult years to deal with the challenges of today.

The Changing Times

There is an alarming trend in our society today. When I was growing up the formula was to go to school, get a good job, save a bunch of money and retire happy. This formula doesn't work anymore. Today's economy creates and dismantles entire industries in the time it takes to get a college education. Skills considered valuable one day are obsolete the next. The most important skill we can teach our children today is adaptability.

The promise of job security doesn't really exist for them with outsourcing, downsizing and automation. Social security will not likely be there in their futures either. The world is changing and a different formula is required to adapt. I am not going to claim to know what that formula is. However, I do claim that adaptability is key in order to be able to figure it out. I will explain how to empower your kids with the crucial skills of adaptability. Adults should learn this mindset as well. The only constant is change. It is guaranteed.

A century ago, most people were small business owners. We were farmers, shop owners or self-employed service people. With the industrial revolution and the rise of huge companies, it became the norm to work for someone else. We became factory workers and office workers. Now with the advent of the internet and 24/7 information access for everyone, small business is rising again. Entrepreneurs are increasing in number. The power is returning to the individual. The rules are changing again. If we continue to expect our kids to succeed by the same formulas we followed, we may find disappointment instead.

You can wish it were the way it used to be. You can complain about change when it affects your job or your income, but it will happen anyway. Children today need to learn to deal with inevitable change, even when it is unpredictable, *especially* when it is unpredictable. How do you teach your kids this incredibly important skill? Experience. The more you try, the more you learn and the more perspectives and angles you have to approach a new situation. Read the quote at the beginning of this chapter again and think about if for a minute. Experience is critical.

The Different Faces of Experience

There are several kinds of experiences. Some are positive for development and some are not and can actually hurt development. Negative experiences that cause early life stress, like abuse, neglect, and major loss can actually damage brain circuits that deal with stress. These can lead to depression and anxiety disorders later in life. Even though some people seem to turn these into incredible springboards for success, I'm obviously not advocating this type of experience or suggesting that you seek it out. The focus of this chapter is on positive experiences that will optimize brain performance.

There are two kinds of positive experiences.

1. New experiences that require learning
2. Practical experience that leads to mastery

The first type, new experiences, leads to mental adaptability. Neuroscientists use the term 'plasticity', which refers to the plastic nature of the brain. Plastic, in this sense, means flexible and able to change. The brain is a very plastic and adaptable organ and new experiences enhance this.

The second type of experience is referring to repetition. A professional athlete is a good example of using the power of repetitive experience. Essentially this is practice in order to master the art of a given skill set. I will discuss this type of experience in detail as well as it applies to optimizing brain performance.

Maximizing our kids' potential requires focus on both types of experience. They both have advantages but must not be confused with each other. Often times someone might work the same job for many years and claim '10 years of experience.' However, there is a big difference between 10 years of experience and 1 year of experience 10 times. If you continue to do the same thing repeatedly, are you really getting more experience? You are certainly developing mastery but not likely getting any new experiences. Balancing these is two types of experience is the key.

Fail Forward

People get comfortable with repetitive experience because mastery decreases the chance of failure, while seeking new experiences guarantees some level of failure. What many people don't realize is that failure is good. Failure is important. You must allow your kids to make mistakes in order to give them the joy of learning for themselves. Some things can't be taught. They must be learned through experience. They must be acquired *slowly* so that the outcomes are fully understood and appreciated. We all want to save our kids from the pain of failure. For many situations, this is okay. I'm not suggesting that you force them to reinvent the wheel. However, there are many lessons that they simply must learn on their own. Let them.

The typical self-made millionaire in the United States tried and failed an average of 16 different businesses before they finally succeeded. Whether or not financial success is your goal, the point is that failure is an important part of the formula on the way to a successful life. Unless you are putting your kids in harm's way or risking serious injury by allowing your kids to fail, just let them try. They will become stronger and more successful adults for the experience of it.

Let's look at some successes through failure.

Over 400 publishers rejected Jack Canfield and Mark Victor Hanson before one agreed to take a chance and publish "Chicken Soup for the Soul." This is now one of the best selling book series of all time.

Colonel Sanders visited over 1,000 restaurants before he found one that would make his chicken recipe. When would most people have given up? After three rejections? Ten rejections?

Thomas Edison tried about 400 ways to make a light bulb before he found the one that worked. After about 350 tries, an assistant asked him why he continued when he had failed so many times. His reply was "Young man, I have not failed at all. I have simply determined hundreds of ways that it won't work."

I could fill a book with these types of success through failure stories. They all could have given up. However, every failure was a new learning experience that fed their eventual success. The point is, let your kids fail. Kids are always coming up with a grand idea that you know won't work. Don't discourage them. Let them figure it out for themselves. They may actually surprise you with their ingenuity.

When I was about 10 years old, my best friend and I came up with a plan. We were going to dig an intricate system of tunnels in his back yard. We had it all planned out with secret rooms and passages. It was going to be the best fort ever made. Of course, it was doomed to failure but we didn't know that and we tried. We dug a pit about 4 feet deep and 3 feet across that was to be the main entrance before we realized we wouldn't be able to do it. Beside the fact that his parents weren't too happy about the hole, the tunnels just weren't going to hold up. Nevertheless, this was a valuable experience. We learned something about trying an idea. We also learned something about hard work.

An upside of this experience is that we turned that hole into a hidden grave for a 'haunted backyard' that we produced on Halloween. We produced and incredible backyard of ghosts flying from trees, monsters jumping out of graves and all kinds of cool stuff. We charged neighborhood kids three pieces of candy to go through the yard. This way we were able to earn all the candy we would have made from trick-or-treating by having a blast putting on the haunted backyard. We might never have even thought of it without the failed tunnel project.

An old adage says 'when one door closes, another one opens.' If fear of failure paralyzes you then your kids will learn this mentality as well. Then, they will miss so many of life's opportunities. It is very important to let your kids know that it is okay to fail. Let them struggle a little with things. Don't try to do everything for them. They must learn that it's okay to fail and that if they keep trying they will get it.

This is something that you must role model as well. Let them see you fail. We all fail at things. Don't try to appear perfect in your kids' eyes. Eventually they will figure out that you are not. The more comfortable you are in your own missed efforts and the more they see you accept them but not give up, the better off they will be.

Persistence is Key

Another old adage of 'if at first you don't succeed, try, try again' is probably one of the most important simple life lessons that there is. There is so much wisdom in our history. Unfortunately, things like that get to be so cliché that we start to ignore them. How many adults give up after one or two tries at something? The excuse is usually "I tried that, it didn't work for me" or "I'm not any good at that." What kind of message does that send to our kids? What if Michael Jordan would have said, "I'm not good enough at basketball" when his coach cut him from his high school team? He would have robbed the world of his talents as a beautiful player.

No one is a master of anything when they first get started. Many parents understand this when it come to their kids. We know that with effort our kids can learn whatever skill or lesson they are trying to. However, many parents don't role model this very well. Many people think that once we reach adulthood we have already figured out all the things we can and can't do. We become resistant to trying new things because of the fear of failure. Then we are not prepared to deal with change when it sneaks up on us. This is probably the single biggest thing that holds adults back from reaching *their* potential. Teach your kids not to fear failure, but to embrace challenges and learn from them. Teach them to try again. This is an incredibly important life skill for their success.

The take-home message for all of this is to challenge your kids and allow them to challenge themselves. Don't do everything for them. Children who are comfortable with challenges know that they will eventually prevail. They know that they have what it takes to overcome. They will take this skill forward in life and approach situations with optimism that many will approach with stress and uncertainty.

Don't Push

A fine line that we, as parents, need to understand is when to challenge and when to back off. This is most likely to be a problem when your kids show a great affinity for something; when they are good at a sport, an instrument, or an academic subject. You want to encourage their talents because you can see them excelling in that area.

Kids do need to be pushed a little, especially if they are the type that will slack off when left to their own. However, pushing them too hard in an area will usually backfire. They may be good for a while but will eventually rebel against what they are being pushed to do when they begin to explore independence.

There is a big difference between challenging kids and pushing them. When we challenge kids, we are setting them up for success using the small steps that I talk about below. We are leading them, but allowing them to find their own way. If they fail the challenge, they might feel a little down, but you must ensure that they don't feel disappointment from you. You help them figure out where they went wrong and try again, maybe with a different approach.

On the other hand, when we push kids we are using more pressure to get them to succeed in an area we have defined for them. If they fail in this context, they will feel your disappointment. They will base their desire to succeed on how you react and not how they see themselves.

We must find a way to create success in the areas that they show natural ability without the immense pressure to win or compete. I am very opposed to a must win attitude in kids. I see this in my sports experience and it is just not helping their long-term potential. Don't get me wrong. Competition is important. Life is full of competition and kids need to learn how to compete. However, they should not learn 'a win at all costs' attitude or fear that they will lose your respect if they don't win. As I discussed earlier in the chapter, they must know that it is OK to fail so that they won't be afraid to try.

If you are interested in specific advice about raising athletes and the balance between competitive and cooperative attitudes, I recommend a great book by Jim Thompson called, "The Double Goal Coach." Jim started an organization called the Positive Coaching Alliance and has recruited the support of highly successful coaches, including the NBA legend, Phil Jackson. He has an incredible philosophy of how to balance coaching to win and the development of individuals. The book is great for both coaches and parents of athletic children.

Create Small Successes

Challenging your kids appropriately requires a balance between success and failure. In order to develop their confidence they must overcome the challenges some of the time. You must ensure that they encounter situations where they will succeed. At the same time, they must also experience failure for reasons described above. This is a difficult balancing act for a parent.

As a soccer coach I deal with this balancing act all of the time. I will give you an analogy from how I teach players to succeed in sports that you can generalize to your own situation. When I am teaching players a new skill or trying to get them to improve a skill, I follow a very simple format. Let's use shooting the ball at the goal for example.

I show the kids how to shoot the ball with the correct technique. I show them how to strike the ball with their shoelaces, with their toe-down and ankle locked, and how to swing from the knee and the hip and how to follow through.

Then it is their turn to strike a ball. But I don't start out by having them take on a defender and shoot on goal. They are learning the technique. I want to create success so that I can build on it later. I want them to practice and demonstrate the technique with no pressure. There are no defenders, not even a goal to shoot on that they might miss and feel bad. I simply want them to strike the ball. This ensures the highest chance for successful development of the technique.

When they get comfortable with that then it is time to move to a goal. Since I have already worked with them to get them striking the ball with the correct technique, I am confident they can hit the target. There is still no outside pressure. They only have the pressure of their own mind, which I try to keep at a minimum. This will build their confidence level inch by inch.

The next step is to introduce some time or space pressure. Maybe they have to strike 10 balls in 30 seconds. I don't want a goal that they can't achieve, but one that they have to work at a little. Again, I am building more success on their prior accomplishments and adding a little complexity each time. This makes the small successes more rewarding.

Then I will introduce the pressure of a 'passive' defender. Another player or I will put light pressure on them before they can shoot on goal. Finally, they will get live pressure from a defender and need to use everything they have learned in a game-like situation.

Each step creates success before the difficulty of the next challenge is increased. They are building from simple to complex situations, each getting closer to 'real life'. I could just show them the technique and throw them into live play but the challenge of this would be too great and the likelihood of success would be too small.

This is a very basic method of building from the simple to the complex but so many times parents expect too much from their kids too soon. We get down on them when they don't succeed. Sometimes we expect them to get the whole process all at once.

A player may master the above process in a single practice session or it may take an entire season. Different kids will move to mastery at different speeds. An important thing to understand is that the amount of time it takes to get to mastery does not predict the level of mastery they will eventually achieve. Some kids might be naturally talented in an area but actually progress too quickly and not master the basics. Others may struggle at each step but be better for it because they spend more time with each basic principle. Sometimes the kids that move more slowly end up with a deeper sense of understanding.

I'm not saying that we shouldn't create expectations. This is part of instilling a challenge. It's okay to hold kids accountable to perform. However, we must only hold them accountable to a reasonable level of performance at each level of mastery. When we expect too much we destroy their confidence and their desire to push on.

This is not an analogy only applicable to sports. This is applicable to any skill that your child wants to possess. Building from simple to complex allows them to take what they know and apply it to a new situation. It makes a learning experience positive and manageable instead of stressful and overwhelming. The important thing is to focus on creating success at each stage.

Creating success means allowing them to figure it out on their own and at a reasonable pace. If we do it for them, there is no opportunity for success. If we push them too hard, they will not be ready for the next step. This is perhaps the most difficult aspect of coaching for me. I want to teach them so much, but it will take years to do it. Parenting and coaching from this perspective requires another level of patience. It requires patience in the moment and patience to move slowly toward the vision of eventual mastery.

Building Brain Circuits

Working from simple to complex also optimizes how the brain learns. The initial exposure of the new experience comes in a non-threatening, low-pressure environment. They experience a situation without stress. The initial experience creates a placeholder in their brain. Then secondary experiences already have some context to fit into and will have more value. Slowly building from simple to complex will strengthen brain circuits and facilitate mastery.

This comes back to the balance between new and repetitive experiences. Kids need some repetition with predictability for comfort and they need challenges with variety for growth. The degree of which will be optimal depends completely on the child. All children are unique and each has a different set point that is ideal for them to get the most of a situation. Unlike, good nutrition and physical activity, which are good for all kids, you are the expert on the amount of predictability that your child needs. Still, there are some basic concepts that you should think about.

The Benefits of Routines

Routines are important for kids. Routines provide a sense of predictability that is incredibly important in a child's life. Children need to feel some sense of predictability in order to feel safe and in control of their situations. Adults are not that different in this regard. We all want to have a good idea of what to expect each day. However, children's routines are mostly imposed upon them where adults typically have some level of control.

Younger kids need to know what to expect when they get to class in the morning. They need to know that you will be there to pick them up from school or that someone will be there to meet them when they get off the bus. They need to know that they can feel safe and unthreatened at home.

Too much unpredictability can be damaging. In fact, studies show that the worst kind of stress is the feeling that you are not in control of your own life. This is true for adults as well as kids. But kids are more susceptible to long-term modifications of brain circuits that control stress. I'm not talking about everyday stressors, but those that leave kids fearful because they don't know what to expect from abusive adults in their lives. These types of experiences can harm brain circuits and increase later life risk of depression or anxiety problems.

Variety Improves Attention

Variety is also incredibly important in kids' lives. They need continual challenges in order to grow and improve. If everything in a child's life is always predictable then they have no reason to think creatively and they can become less attentive to their environment. The brain is always scanning the environment to see what is changing. There is no reason to pay attention to things that are the same because they have already been 'tagged' in the mind. The brain will pay attention to things that it perceives to have value or to be threatening. It will ignore everything else, especially if the environment is not changing and there is no reason to re-evaluate it.

Environments that are unchanging cause the brain to slowly become less attentive. It becomes conditioned not to expect anything new. Environments that mix it up a little keep the brain on guard, attentive and alert.

Variety is the Spice of Life

Do you remember the discussions in the chapter on physical activity about the formation of new brain cells? Well it turns out that an interesting environment does that as well. Environments that change and offer new opportunities for exploration promote brain cell growth in the hippocampus, the same region improved by exercise. As I discussed before, this region is involved in attention, learning and memory, and response to stress. Brain cell growth in the hippocampus, induced by exercise and an interesting environment, is protective against stress, anxiety and depression.

In addition, new environments also lead to growth in other brain areas that control 'higher functions,' such as problem solving, social behavior and language skills. Even brain regions involved in fine motor skill control benefit from changing and interesting environments, leading to improved coordination.

Much of this information comes from studies with animals in controlled environments. However, there is data from human studies that support these conclusions as well. For example, studies show that un-enriched environments during elementary school years lead to lower performance in school.

Challenges Make Kids Think

What are some examples of interesting environments? Typically, this environment continually presents kids with new challenges or things to explore. Environments that require active participation and problem solving, not passive participation like most television shows. For example, visiting new places, playing different games or puzzles and reading different stories all add to the brain's interest in an environment. Essentially anything that requires the brain to re-evaluate the things in the environment promotes interest and exploration.

There is an African tribal saying that 'when the belly is full, the brain doesn't work.' What this is referring to is that if all of your needs are met then there is no reason to think. If you have enough food and shelter there is no reason to think creatively to survive. Of course, today, most of us have enough food and shelter and this is not the source of our challenges. Still, continual challenges help kids to make new brain connections.

Challenges force learning and employ our creative side. They force us to use our imagination to find solutions. This actually creates new brain connections. The brain is a network of neurons that communicate with each other through contacts called 'synapses.' A single neuron can have hundreds to thousands of synapses with other neurons. You can follow a brain signal from a thought or action from one neuron to the next, down a pathway of connections. The more synapses that form, the more paths there are to get from one place to another. Challenges create the formation of new synapses and pathways to provide new solutions to get things done.

Not only that but the more these pathways are used by tasks, thoughts or challenges, the stronger they get. This is where new experience and repetition complement each other. A new connection, made by a new experience, might start out very weak. If it is never used again it will actually 'de-connect' and the synapse will disappear. However if a new connection is used repeatedly it will get stronger. The synapse becomes very stable and able to move thought signals along the pathway much faster and more reliably.

Think of it like a system of roads. Many of the freeways that we have today started out as trails. As more traffic began to use them, especially with the advent of the automobile, they became dirt roads. Eventually they became important enough routes to pave, which increased the speed and the reliability of the route. As more and more traffic 'voted' for the importance of these routes, they became highways and then freeways. Unused trails overgrew and disappeared.

The brain works the same way. Pathways form all the time through creating new connections. Those that are useful get used and are improved and strengthened. Those that don't prove useful whither and fade. Challenges and new experiences simply increase the rate of creation of new pathways. In addition, repetition and practice increase the efficiency and strength of the relevant pathways.

A child continually challenged with new learning experiences will have a much greater chance of creating useful brain pathways because they are creating new ones all the time. A child that gets 'stuck in a rut' with very few challenges will not create as many new pathways and is not likely to end up with as many useful pathways that are strengthened over time. They may get good at doing things they practice but they may not have the adaptability to take a different route when necessary.

Learning does not have to be a formal lesson. Just visiting new places, seeing different perspectives, reading books that take them to new worlds or provide new ways of thinking are all valuable learning opportunities.

This is not to say that all experiences are good. Threats at a young age can create very strong pathways that are difficult to dismantle later. For example, abusive or life threatening situations from living in dangerous environments can create pathways in the stress system that can have long-term effects. These types of experiences can lead to increased odds of depression or anxiety in adults because the pathways associated with negative emotions are so well entrenched. Of course, all parents want to protect their kids from life threatening situations for reasons that are good in the moment and later on.

Emotion Strengthens the Path

In addition to heavy use strengthening a pathway, they also strengthen by importance. A new pathway will stabilize very quickly if created by an important situation. If a child experiences something simultaneous to invoking emotion, then that pathway stabilizes more strongly. This is the same reason we usually remember what we were doing when we heard tragic news that touched us emotionally. I will share one story from my own past that created a very strong pathway in my own brain.

I did not grow up in any kind of threatening environment. I grew up in a safe and caring home and didn't have to worry about any kind of survival issues. Nevertheless, one day when I was about 7 years old, my parents took my sister and me for a hike through the woods near our house. We were walking along having a good time out in nature when all of a sudden I stepped in a hornet's nest in an old bike tire. Hornets swarmed us and I was stung about 12 times. I created a strong pathway in my brain that hornets equal pain. Unfortunately, a couple of years later my best friend and I did the same thing and I was stung multiple times again. Not only was the 'hornet' pathway already strong because of the context it was created in (with the emotion of fear), but now it was further strengthened by a second experience. For the rest of my childhood, adolescence and even into early adulthood I had a fear of bees, hornets and anything similar. I was finally able to weaken that pathway with repeated exposure to bees without being stung but it took a long time.

My point is that the context that creates a pathway has a lot to do with its initial strength. Pathways created under emotional conditions are much stronger because they are deemed important by the brain. This can happen in the context of positive emotions like love or joy; or negative emotions like fear or anger. This is why people learn much better when they are having a good time. Kids learn better, when they are having fun. The brain interprets whatever it is learning as important because it is coupled with a strong emotion of joy.

My sister-in-law is a schoolteacher and has always been a proponent of teaching through games. She focuses mostly on board games that promote math skills, problem solving and logical thinking. These games work because of the skill they require. However, they also work because of the emotional context in which the skills are learned. When kids are playing games, they are having fun and the brain associates whatever they are doing at the time as important.

To sum all this up, new experiences give your children a number of new brain pathways to apply to future situations. This gives them the best odds of success when they do something new. Repeated experience in the same situation, like practicing a sport or a musical instrument, will physically strengthen the pathways associated with these tasks. Practice will strengthen a pathway to efficiently and expertly accomplish the task.

You may have read this chapter hoping to discover what types of learning experiences are best for intellectual development. The good news is that they are all good. The key is to supply variety in all aspects of kids' lives, coupled with a base routine that keeps them secure. We should expose our kids to as many physical environments as possible. Take them hiking in the outdoors to get a sense of nature. Take them into the big city to get a sense of social environments. Take them to concerts, sporting events, plays, etc. You don't have to spend a lot of money, just enrich their lives. You also should not wait until you think they are old enough to understand these intellectually. Just encountering different stimuli and different environments will promote the development of new brain circuits.

If you have the ability to travel to different cultures, that is invaluable. If not, you can get a lot out of cultural variety near home. Shop and eat in different cultural environments; Chinatown, Mexican town, Little Italy, etc. Exposing kids to different kinds of foods is a great way to introduce variety. The different senses they will stimulate will help generate new connections in the brain.

Exposing them to different kinds of music is another great and easy way to introduce variety; Jazz, Blues, Classical, Country, Rock and Roll, etc. Just try to have a good time with as many different genres as possible. In fact, learning a musical instrument as a child is a very effective way to stimulate the brain. Hundreds of studies have shown an association between learning to play music and various forms of intelligence, especially math and logical thinking skills.

Neither my wife nor I learned to play any instruments as children and both of us really wish that we had. I have personally set a goal to learn to play the piano proficiently by my 45th birthday (about five years from the time of this writing). It is never too late to start, but the earlier the better.

Get Experience—Recap

As I discussed in this chapter, experience is key for optimal development. Here is a quick recap of the main concepts and points.

- Mixing new experiences with old routines and traditions optimizes brain circuits.
- Showing kids that it's okay to fail on initial attempts, helps improve their confidence.
- Encouraging persistence creates a 'can do' attitude.
- Creating small success builds from the simple to the complex.

ACTion™ Plan

Now let's get to some concrete plans that you can use to optimize your kid's brains and empower them with the skills of adaptability and independence. The companion section in the Action Guide will help you design a plan to get the most out of this chapter. You can download it at http://www.thebraincode.com/ActionGuide if you haven't already.

1. **A**ssess the diversity of your kids' current experiences.
   - Do your kids get exposure to a variety of viewpoints or experiences?
   - Are they allowed to fail at things without sensing your disappointment? Do you let them see you fail at things?
   - Are they challenged on a regular basis? Do you encourage persistence to overcome challenges?
2. **C**ommit to mixing up the pot and getting them exposure to new perspectives.
   - Ensure that your kids are exposed to different cultures, even if it's just through different ethnic restaurants, shops, neighborhoods, movies or books.
   - Expose them to a variety of environments, even if they are within your local area.
   - Visit a few new places every year where they will need to explore outside of their comfort zone.
3. Track your progress at introducing new experiences.
   - Repeat step 1. Are you introducing challenges and variety into your kids' lives? Are you encouraging them to take some chances and persist through a challenge?
   - Have you noticed any differences in your kids' insight into different situations? Are they broadening the way they think about things?

- You are doing your kids a huge favor by working on this. Don't forget to celebrate the progress you make.

CHAPTER 6
OWN IT—CREATIVE THINKING

Creative thinking is what sets successful people apart. It is crucial to excelling in any field or environment. We must teach our kids to think for themselves and not just follow the herd if we want them to reach their potential.

Creative thinkers contribute to society in so many ways. They are the artists that fill our worlds with the unique human experience. They are the writers and the filmmakers that produce thought provoking or entertaining works. They are the problem solvers in all professions. They are the ones contributing value to the world. Success absolutely requires creative thinking.

In this chapter, I discuss some simple principles that will help you develop a creative thinker. A big part of thinking creatively is simply thinking independently. We must teach our children to think for themselves and not always rely on input from others, including us as their parents. We must allow our children to realize that they are unique individuals with something to contribute and that their opinions matter. I will discuss some approaches you can use to promote independent and creative thought.

Create It and They will Come

Creative thinking is important because it is how we tap into our unique talent to create value. Society rewards its members for value. If you add value to the lives of others, they will reward you. This is a fact. However, this should not be your sole intent. If you attempt to create value for the sole purpose of self-gain, it will not stand the test of time. We must teach our kids to work from integrity and the genuine intent to contribute, in order to reach their full potential.

The grandfather of motivational speaking, Zig Ziglar, puts it this way.

> "Find a way to help others get what they want and you will get everything that you want."

Many people will cite a universal law that governs 'giving before getting' when describing Zig's famous quote. While this may be true, there is also a much simpler explanation for the wisdom behind this statement, which is that helping others creates value.

We can teach the importance of contributing value in several ways. Team competition is a great way to teach this philosophy. Whether it's academic teams or athletic teams, they reinforce the concept of an individual contributing value for the good of the team. Through these experiences our kids learn that by doing their best they will be helping themselves by helping those around them.

Once these lessons are learned, they can contribute value as they grow, through entertainment, education or service. However, to truly make a difference they must be able to think creatively. They must be able to find a unique perspective or an original approach to solve problems. This is what we must teach them while they are young.

Forget the Formulas

I have another analogy from my sports experience to describe the value of creative thinking.

It is no secret that the United States is not a men's soccer power in the world. We have improved dramatically over the past couple of decades but we have a long way to go. However, it may surprise you that statistically, the U.S. is very good at the game. If you track the possession and the technical passing of the U.S. team in recent years they rate very highly. So why aren't they ranked up there with the world powers like Brazil, Germany and Italy? One word. Creativity!

The U.S. has been criticized for the formulaic approach that we use to teach youth sports. We get kids into organized sports at a young age and we teach them the technical aspects of the game. We strip all of the creative drive out of our young players to make them fit the model of team play. We remove the individualism from the game. We are aware of this problem and current coaching clinics address this issue when teaching coaches how to coach.

There is a movement, at least within many youth soccer programs, to nourish creativity in our players.

Let's look at the soccer greats of South America or Europe. How do they learn the game? They learn without coaches! They learn in streets or in back alleys. They learn on beaches and in parks. They just play and make it up as they go. This is where the great players come from. They learn to rely on their own creativity at a young age and figure out the sophisticated technical aspects later.

Look at basketball. The U.S. is dominant in basketball. Professional basketball players have flair and creativity. They entertain crowds with their incredible showmanship. Where do they learn to play? Most professional basketball players are not mentored at a young age by a sophisticated coach. They learn to play in the schoolyards and on the street; shooting hoops in the driveway or at the neighborhood park.

The theme here is that developing creativity requires letting kids figure it out for themselves. It requires that adults don't impose their 'my way or the highway' views onto kids' impressionable minds. It means just stepping back and letting them play.

In fact, the American Academy of pediatrics released a statement in the fall of 2006 that backs that up. The Academy cites many studies that tout the importance of free and unstructured play. This type of play draws out kids' creativity. It puts them in charge of their own worlds.

We hear the expression 'think outside of the box' all the time. But it's not easy to think outside the box when all of your training and education was inside the box. We need to know when to simply let kids create.

I'm not suggesting that coaching or teaching kids to do things 'right' does not have value. However, sometimes we are so caught up in teaching them the method that we forget there are other routes to the same solution. A common mistake that many coaches, teachers and parents make is that we 'teach to the lesson.' We design lessons to teach specific skills required to become better players, students or people. But we should never lose sight that the ultimate goal is performance in the game or in life, not in the lesson. Many times, we correct kids for not following the goals of the lesson, even if their action would have been the right thing to do in reality.

I have had many occasions where kids have proven me wrong. Working with my own kids at chores or tasks around the house or working with the kids that I coach on the soccer field. I will be showing them or telling them the method they 'need' to use and trying to correct them from deviating from it when all of a sudden, they accomplished the task by their own method. I am left scratching my head thinking 'why didn't I think of that.'

This is not just an approach for sports, but for all areas of life. Let kids create. Let them dream. Let them amaze and astound you with their genius.

Please don't ever tell them that it is impossible for them to do something one way just because you don't see how it can be done.

On this topic, I have interviewed one of my former mentors and master coach who has successfully drawn out the best in generations of his players. Cliff McCrath is the head soccer coach at Seattle Pacific University and one of the most winning college soccer coaches in the nation. His teams won five national championships and he is in the United States Soccer Hall of Fame. Cliff is also an ordained minister and spiritual leader in the Seattle area. Follow the link below to listen to my interview with Cliff as he explains how he gets the best out of people. http://www.thebraincode.com/offers.

Invasion of the School System

Nowhere is formulaic teaching a bigger problem than in our school systems. Current policies force teachers to adopt curriculum for the sole purpose of improving students' performance on national standardized tests. These policies increasingly frustrate teachers, keeping their own unique perspectives and philosophies behind bars.

This is a very dangerous movement for our country in general. Today the United States is still a world leader on the economic stage. We are still leading in creativity and production, but how long will this last? When will the creative minds in China and India start outsourcing their menial labor to the United States? When will our formulaic methods of teaching, which rob both teachers and children of creative thinking, catch up to us?

Teaching to the test may seem to be working on paper. Our kids may be regurgitating useless facts at increased proficiency, but I strongly believe that this is a huge problem. We are teaching kids to be sheep. We must get involved with our schools to reverse this trend.

We are taking public schools for granted. We assume that it is the government's job to educate our kids. It is their job to give them the necessary tools to succeed in life. After all, we pay our taxes. Well, it's not working. We, as parents, must get involved in our public education systems. Find your passion and help your kids. Find an area that you can contribute value to the schools in your community.

Perhaps you are good at mechanical things and can help kids learn how things work and help develop their inquisitive minds. Perhaps you have artistic or musical flair and can cater to their imaginative side. Maybe you have expertise in sports and can help kids learn sportsmanship and teamwork. Many parents have skills that they would be happy to share but just don't know how to get involved. We assume that the system has it all worked out and doesn't need us. I can assure you that this is not true. Call up your child's teacher or principal or other community organizer and offer a little time. They would love it. The more we as parents get involved, the more our kids will benefit.

I realize that I have harshly criticized schools throughout this book. I have cited the atrocious nature of school nutrition, the problems of disappearing physical education programs and now, the formulaic approach we are taking in the classroom. I want to be clear that most educators, especially the teachers directly interacting with our student's are not the problem. The problem is policy, which comes down to budget constraints, which ultimately comes down to the lack of value that we, as communities, give to our education system. Simply thinking a little creatively yourself on ways to get involved will go a long way.

In the late 1700's, the English philosopher Edmund Burke, said something like,

"The only thing necessary for evil to prevail is for good men to do nothing."

Although the exact quote has been lost, the wisdom lives on. I'm not suggesting a grand evil plot but the point is that when good people remain spectators then systems decay. Most of us are currently standing back and watching our education system erode. We must take action. Throughout this book, I have linked out to interviews with movers and shakers. In each of these I have asked them, what parents can do to help in various areas. If we all find one area that we care about and do something, the impact will be amazing.

I'm sure you've heard the saying "if you're not with us, you're against us." Personally, I don't buy into that philosophy. It is unrealistic to expect everyone to take up every good cause. We simply don't have the time or resources. However, if you align your passion with a single cause you will be surprised how effective you can be. Don't get involved out of guilt. That won't work. Get involved with something you enjoy. Find a way to turn whatever passion you have into contributing value to your community. We can all do something that makes us proud.

The Path of Least Resistance

A developed society, like ours, channels us down the path of least resistance. We have systems in place to help people move through life. We start school when we are very young. If we do what we are told, we get reasonable grades and get into college or find a good job right out of high school. We continue to follow the path carved out by thousands that have gone before us without questioning whether we are on the right road.

Most people end up in a job that they come to dislike but don't have courage to leave because it would mean blazing a new path. It would mean financial insecurity and stepping outside of their comfort zone. This becomes increasingly difficult once we have started a family and have others depending upon us. So we continue to follow the path and plug along.

The minority of people figure out what they love to do early in life and make a career doing it. Some figure it out later in life and make the necessary changes to get on the right path. This is what we must instill in our kids. We must get them to ask questions and figure out what they truly want to do. We must help them identify their own voice and unique talents and let them take the road less traveled. If we don't encourage them to find their own voice then our social systems will assign one to them.

Talk to Their Brains

Encouraging creativity starts at home. This is an area where many of us could use help. It is so easy to speak to our kids in dogmatic ways that inhibit creative thinking. Most of us do this all of the time without even realizing it. We even do it when we have the best intentions.

I will use an example from my own coaching efforts to illustrate what I'm talking about. Let's say a player scores a goal by shooting the ball with power and accuracy into the corner. I could say 'great goal' or 'awesome shot', which are both positive things to say but they are also judgmental. I am giving them my opinion of their shot. Instead, I could say 'wow, you put that ball right in the corner!' Still supportive and positive but it requires them to interpret my comment as good or bad. The message they get that it was a great shot comes from their own self-talk, not mine. This will foster independent thinking and bolster creativity.

This is a very subtle point that many of us don't really pay attention to. I know that I didn't realize I was doing it until someone brought it to my attention. The bottom line is that we should try to get kids evaluating their own actions instead of giving them our opinions as much as possible. This leads to independent and creative thinking that will serve them well as they grow. It will get them creating their own self-image instead of relying on the image cast upon them by other people.

Don't Lie

There is another reason to avoid positive judgmental statements. Many of us tend to over-praise our kids in an attempt to make them feel better or increase their confidence. When kids are very young they believe you when say "great job," even when it's not true.

As they get a little older and self-aware of their own abilities, these well-meaning words of encouragement can have the opposite effect. If you continually tell your child "good job" when they know they are not doing that well, you will lose credibility. They will know that you are praising them out of obligation or trying to make them feel better and then you will become the 'boy that cried wolf.' Your words, although kind, will become empty and meaningless.

In addition, if you are in the continual habit of praising your children they will become dependent upon it. They will look for praise all of the time. They will require it to feel good about their accomplishments. They will not find enough satisfaction in knowing that they did a good job themselves. Praise is a judgment of them and they become reliant on other people positively judging them.

Using specific statements gets around this problem because you are always telling the truth. You leave the interpretation up to them. If they are indeed doing a good job then they will tell themselves that. You can usually find something redeeming about their performance or behavior, even when they are having a bad day. Speaking to that specifically is a great way to highlight the positive.

Chick Moorman is a speaker and an author who has talked about this extensively. He has several great books on this topic, including 'Parent Talk' and 'The Ten Commitments' that go into great detail on this philosophy. You can also access an interview that I did with Chick through http://www.thebraincode.com/offers.

Project Inward

Stephen Covey also talks at length about this principle in his renowned book "The 7 Habits of Highly Effective People." He uses the terminology of the 'social mirror.'

Stephen describes how children look to the outside world for feedback on their own self-image. They require others to project upon them the image that they have of themselves. However, as they grow they need to become more and more self-projecting. They need to develop self-image from the inside and not always let others project upon them from the outside. Many adults still have problems doing this. We constantly look for the approval of others. The more you can teach your kids to become independent of this the better off they will be.

Denis Waitley, former US Olympic team sports psychologist, say's it this way,

"Be a thermostat, not a thermometer."

Meaning set your own temperature. Don't just respond to the temperature of your environment. Control your own thoughts. Don't always allow other people to project your thoughts and opinions for you.

All of these incredible minds are making the same point in their own way. To heed their advice on this subject is one of the best things you can do to develop your child's independence. I also touched on another aspect of this subject in chapter 4, in 'downtime for the mind.' I remind you here that in addition to the type of speak we put into their minds, allowing them the downtime to speak to their own minds will consolidate their self-talk and accelerate their progress.

I remember when I first started to work consciously on my own self-talk. When I was growing up, I was incredibly sensitive to the opinions that other people had of me. Most of us are. Then I met a friend in college who was a teammate of mine on the soccer team. He immediately impressed me with his ability to shed off the opinions of other people. He was not anti-social. In fact, he was very popular on the team and around campus. But he didn't care what other people thought of him. He was very good at self-projecting his own image.

I didn't think of it in those terms back then but I did try to model his abilities. It is not something that is easy to do after a lifetime of allowing others to impose their image on you. I tried to stay aware of it and worked hard for several years before getting to a point where I was comfortable with my own self-projections. I got to the point where my opinions of myself outweighed those of others around me. I still care what other people think, we all do. But I don't let other people's opinions of me determine what I do and don't do. I don't let other people stop me from pursuing my dreams, which is the ultimate goal that I am trying to convey here.

The faster we can teach our kids to get to this point, the better off they will be. This will not happen overnight. Hyper-concern about other people's opinions is part of being a kid, especially in the teenage and early dating years. However, if you keep trying to develop this character trait it will sink below the surface and give them the power to draw on it when they are ready.

So many adults never really learn how to self-project. They let other people's opinions hold them back. They don't act on desires or goals because they are worried what people will think. I don't want this for my own kids and I hope that you don't want it for yours either.

Recap

I hope that this chapter has given you some unique insights into how you can build creative and independent thinking in your kids. Here is a quick recap of the main points.

- Creative thinking allows contribution of unique talents and value.

- When teachers/coaches are required to stick to formulas creativity is hurt.

- Encouraging kids to evaluate themselves leads to independence.

ACTion™ Plan

Let's get down to the process of moving forward. Again, to get the most out of this section you can refer to the specific plan in the companion section of the Action Guide, which you can download from http://www.thebraincode.com/ActionGuide. Due to the more abstract nature of this chapter, specific steps will leave more room for your interpretation.

1. Assess how you are encouraging independent and creative thinking in your kids.

    - Do you catch yourself using a 'my way or the highway' approach when dealing with your kids? Are you a 'control freak'?

    - Do you do too much for your kids when you know that they could do it themselves?

    - Do you allow your kids to find their own solutions to problems?

    - Do you use language that encourages kids to evaluate their own behavior?

    - Track yourself for an entire day.

2. **C**ommit to encouraging your kids to think for themselves.

   - Next time you see your kids struggling to do something or asking for your help, ask yourself if they really need it. Do they just want you to do it for them?

   - Try to use language that encourages kids to evaluate themselves. Here are some examples of alternatives to judgmental statements like "good job":

   To a young child learning to color—"You stayed completely within the lines!"

   To an elementary school kid that brought home a perfect test—"You got every single question correct!"

   To a baseball player that hit a home run—"You smacked that ball so hard it hit the fence!"

   - For more help with this listen to the interview with Chick Moorman at http://www.thebraincode.com/offers

3. **T**rack your progress and celebrate success.

   - Repeat the assessment in step 1. Track yourself again after consciously working on this for a month. Are you doing better?

   - Is there anything that you have tried that is working well or anything that needs to be modified? Make necessary changes.

- Celebrate the successes that you have had in this area and keep pushing on.

The next chapter will discuss empowering your kids with beliefs in themselves.

CHAPTER 7
SEE IT TO BELIEVE IT—DREAM BIG DREAMS

The last topic I want to discuss relates to having goals and dreams. All kids should dream freely without the barriers of adult opinion. When do we learn that things are unrealistic? When we are kids, we think that anything is possible. Who tells us that they are not and what qualifications do they have? We all want to protect our kids from disappointment but we should be careful not to stifle their ambition and their creativity in the process.

This chapter is really the culmination of everything before it. This topic is about utilizing the brain's infrastructure that the preceding chapters built. Dreaming big dreams is uniquely a human trait. The ability to see ourselves in the future and to achieve a purpose in life requires a level of consciousness that only we have. This is what I meant by your child's birthright that I mentioned in the opening pages of this book. A human birthright to live with purpose, to contribute values and to achieve our full potential that no one has the right to steal. We are blessed to live in the free world and seek our birthright and we should feel obligated to teach our kids to do just that.

Believe It

It all comes down to beliefs. What we as adults believe is possible or probable is very different from what kids believe. But we shouldn't be so sure that we are right and they are wrong. The funny thing about beliefs is that we actually believe them! It sounds obvious. However, we must realize that many of the beliefs we have today are not true. History tells us this is the case. We don't know what we don't know. Think about that for a second. How do you know when you don't know something? You can't. We must be careful not to hold our beliefs too strongly when they don't serve us well.

We Don't Know what We Don't Know

I like to use the 'world is flat' belief to illustrate this point. It wasn't that long ago that we all believed the world was flat. We *knew* the world was flat. Anyone who claimed otherwise was just crazy. That was only about 600 years ago. Now we know that we were all just ignorant.

In my professional field of molecular biology, I witness discoveries every year that unveil different systems in the human body. Systems that are critical for our function but that we didn't even know existed a year ago. The question then becomes, how much don't we know about how the world works. It is estimated that our knowledge doubles every 5 years.

How much is left to discover? We are only scratching the surface of the truth about our world. We know so little.

My point in all of this is that we shouldn't be too quick to assume things are impossible, simply because we don't have the current understanding of how they are possible. When it comes to kids, we must be very careful about what messages we put into their minds regarding the feasibility or the probability of their dreams, big or small, coming to fruition. Instead of 'raining on their parade' by telling them they are unlikely to be able to accomplish something, we should be encouraging them to think about how they will do it. We should get them to evaluate their own feasibility. We should feed their dreams not attempt to steal them. One of my favorite quotes relevant to this subject is:

"Those who danced were thought to be quite insane by those that could not hear the music"
—Angela Monet

This statement emphasizes the point that people can have a clear vision of what they are doing even when others nearby don't get it. Just because you can't clearly see your kids' vision, don't assume that they are not realistic.

Avoid Stealing Dreams

Here are some examples that I found in the book "7 Habits of Highly Effective Teens" by Sean Covey. This is a teen version of the famous book with a similar title written by Shawn's father, Stephen Covey. These demonstrate that even people who should know what they are talking about are sometimes quite wrong.

"There is no reason for any individual to have a computer in their home." —1977, Kenneth Olsen, President of Digital Equipment Corporation.

"Airplanes are interesting toys but they have no military value." —1911, Marshall Ferdinand Foch, French Military Strategist and Future WWI Commander.

"Man will never reach the moon regardless of all future scientific advances." —1967 (only 2 years before the moon landing), Dr. Lee De Forest, Father of Radio.

"We don't like their sound. Groups of guitars are on the way out." —1962, Decca Records executives describing the Beatles.

"This 'telephone' has too many shortcomings to be seriously considered as a means of communication." —1876, Western Union, internal memo.

"Nothing of importance happened today." —July 4th, 1776, King George the III describing the signing of the declaration of independence.

"Everything that can be invented has been invented." —1899, Charles Duell, US Commissioner of Patents.

These were smart educated people and leaders in their industries that held these beliefs. Other folks listened to what these people said and adopted their beliefs because they were the experts. Now all of these statements look completely ridiculous to us. How many beliefs do we hold today that history will prove ludicrous?

Society has molded our kids to have certain expectations of their adult lives. Kids are told that they can't do things at very early ages. Much of what they hear relates to careers or making a living. Many kids have dreams that adults just don't see the value in. We cannot see how they will succeed going down those roads so we try to protect them from failure. But we do not have the road map of their future.

We do not squash their dreams deliberately. We are trying to help them understand how reality works. However, we don't completely understand this ourselves, so we should be very careful about setting any roadblocks in our kids' paths. This get's back to the importance of allowing kids to fail forward that I discussed in chapter 5.

A popular story that emphasizes this point is that of the great physicist, Albert Einstein. When Albert was young, he was not a good student. He began speaking at a late age and was a slow learner. In his early adult years, he failed college entrance exams and lost several of his first teaching positions. Many dubbed him 'slow,' 'backwards,' or 'dumb.' How ridiculous does that seem now, knowing what we know? The fact is that he didn't fit the mold.

He didn't perform well inside the formulas that society had laid out for him.

Please don't tell your kids that they have a small chance at anything, because frankly, you don't know. What you think you know is based on your own beliefs and your own experiences. That has no predictive value for your children's potential for accomplishment. The point to all of this is to avoid indoctrinating your kids with dogma. Of course, we need to educate them. Of course, we can share our own viewpoints of the world. We have life experience that they don't have yet and we want to help them learn from our mistakes. However, we must always encourage them to question everything and not to accept anything on blind faith. In the opening chapter, I encourage you, the reader, not to accept anything you read on blind faith. Now I'm asking you to do the same for your kids. Encourage them to formulate their own beliefs.

Find Another Way

Have you seen the movie 'Rudy'? It's a true story about a small kid who always wanted to play football for Notre Dame. But he was too small and not good enough to play for a national power, college football team. He didn't even have the grades to get in. Everyone around him knew that it was just a pipe dream that would never happen. Everyone, that is except Rudy himself.

After years of attending a junior college to get the grades to go to Notre Dame, he finally got in. But there was no way he was going to play for the football team. He convinced the coach to let him show up to practice, only to be beat up by the starters week after week, but he didn't quit.

His resilience and tenacity impressed his teammates and the coaching staff so much that he finally got into the last game of his senior year and actually made a game-winning tackle with only seconds on the clock. He believed in himself when no one else would and he was right!

I listened to an interview with Rudy when I first started writing this book. There was one point that he made that I thought was very insightful. He said that we can all find a way to contribute. Rudy new that he couldn't contribute to the Notre Dame team with athletic ability or football skills. But his heart and his unwavering desire to play inspired his teammates to become better players. He contributed a great deal to the success of that football team, even though he only played for a few seconds of a single game in his entire college career.

The same holds true for anything. Maybe your kids have the ambition to be a singing star but they just don't have the voice. They can still write music. They can still learn vocal styles and teach others. They can still follow their passion and make a difference.

The point is to avoid implanting disempowering beliefs that will sway kids away from their passion just because they don't show the skills that you think are needed. There is always another way to contribute. As long as people find and follow their true passion, they will do great things.

Finding a Voice

Dr. Andrew Weil has a personal statement at the end of his recent book called, "Healthy Aging," that I like very much. He is a scientific man. He believes in evidence-based knowledge, yet his statement illustrates that there is room to believe in that which we can't understand. Here is an excerpt from his book:

"I have learned to rely greatly on intuition, on my inner sense of right and wrong, truth and falsehood. I have cultivated the ability to hear that inner voice, and I test it constantly against my experience and external sources of information. I believe everyone is intuitive; regrettably, our educational systems do not teach us to use that faculty. You must learn it on your own...

...*Either-or* formulations of reality make me uneasy. I much prefer *both-and* formulations. They may seem awkward at first, but they open up many more possibilities and make life more interesting. Try them out...

...I believe in magic and mystery. I am also committed to scientific method and knowledge based on evidence. How can this be? I have told you that I operate from a *both-and* mentality, not an *either-or* one.

...I believe that consciousness is primary, that it is more basic than matter or energy and that it directs evolution of the material universe. I am not interested in trying to prove this conviction or argue it with scientific materialists. The materialists believe that a blind process of natural selection has created the universe, that consciousness is just an 'epiphenomenon' arising from biochemical and electrical activity of the brain. My way of thinking works for me and makes more sense of my experience than other beliefs I have explored..."

I especially like the point in this statement about operating from a both-and philosophy. What this means is that you could hold values and beliefs even if they appear in contradiction with each other. How can this possibly make sense? It goes back to how much we don't know about our world. You judge the feasibility of your own beliefs within the set of rules that you understand. What I am saying is that we don't know all the rules so things that may seem contradictory by our current understanding might not be contradictory after all.

Master magicians prove this all the time. They perform incredible acts on stage that appear to be in contradiction with what we know about reality. However, it is all illusion because they are making us believe that they are doing one thing when in fact they are doing something else. They are simply playing by one set of rules and convincing us that they are using a different set. Making things seem to appear or disappear in front of our eyes. In this context, we know it is a trick but our minds can't understand how it is possible. How many 'real situations' do we incorrectly interpret, simply because we are evaluating them with the wrong set of rules or beliefs?

This is the root of stereotypes that leads to ignorant conclusions. We judge people and situations by our own set of rules that we created over the course of our life. We must realize that we all have sets of rules that are inaccurate.

Choose Empowering Beliefs

The last point I want to make on the subject of beliefs relates to the type of beliefs that we choose to adopt. I encourage you to help your children adopt beliefs that are empowering and dismiss those that are disempowering. Think about it. Why would we believe disempowering things when we don't have proof that they are true? Why would we believe that we couldn't achieve something when it is just as easy to believe that we can? If we don't know whether or not our kids can succeed in their dreams then why choose to believe that they will.

Henry Ford said, "Whether you believe you can or believe you can't, you're right."

What an incredible statement.

We use our beliefs to project into the future based on our experiences of the past. Yet in many cases, there is no predictive value in these past experiences. A simple example of this is evident when watching professional sporting events on TV. The commentators are always pulling out meaningless statistics that drive me nuts. They will make comments like "this team has never come from a 6 point deficit with only 5 minutes left." They might as well be saying, "This team has never won a game on a full moon on a Tuesday when it's raining if the coach had donuts for breakfast." Sometimes we take statistics so far that they become completely irrelevant and meaningless. We learn in grade school that if you flip a coin and it turns up heads the first nine times it is still a 50-50 chance of heads or tails on the next flip. The previous history of the coin has no bearing on predicting the future.

As parents, we must be careful not to predict the chance of our kid's success based on our unique experiences. They are not us. Times are different and the factors that contributed to our past are not identical to those that our kids face today.

Tony Robbins, a famous motivational speaker, has some great taglines. One that I have put a lot of thought into is "the past does not equal the future." However, by adopting disempowering beliefs about the future we increase the chance that they become self-fulfilling. We could just as easily project empowering beliefs and increase the chance that success will unfold instead of failure.

Am I suggesting that what we believe can actually affect the future? Yes I am. Let me tell you why. First, many people believe that consciousness drives reality. The previous statement by Dr. Weil supports that viewpoint. A large portion of the self-help industry is founded on that principle. I don't know whether this is true, but I certainly don't discount this possibility. I want to believe it. After all, as I stated above, there is still so much we just don't understand about our world. I do not discount possibilities simply because I cannot understand how they work. In fact, I believe that to do so would be arrogant. However, I'm not describing anything so mystical when I state that beliefs can influence the future.

I am referring to how your own beliefs and self-talk actually rewire your brain so that you pay attention to things that support your point of view. The stronger you believe something the stronger the connections in the brain will become that support that belief. I already discussed how pathways in the brain get entrenched through experience. Well, beliefs do the same thing. Except in this case, pathways are being entrenched by 'internal experience' created by your thoughts and beliefs instead of 'external experience' created by your environment.

When these pathways get entrenched, they essentially become the path of least resistance to interpret what is going on around you. If you believe something to be true then your brain will attempt to make your experience fit that belief. You will react to situations based on your beliefs in a way that will perpetuate your beliefs. You have essentially wired the connections in your brain to come up with a predetermined conclusion.

Your brain is constantly filtering out the unimportant stuff in your environment and focusing on the important stuff. Well, the things that you tag as important are largely dependent upon your beliefs. Your beliefs influence what you subconsciously choose to focus on in your environment. Your mind will interpret your environment in a way that supports your beliefs.

A very exciting area of brain research that applies to this concept revolves around 'mirror neurons.' We have neurons in our brain that fire in an attempt to predict what other people in our environment will do. For example if you pick up a glass and take a drink, the neurons in your brain fire in a certain pattern to control that. Now, if you watch someone else pick up a glass and take a drink a very similar neuron-firing pattern happens in your brain. Your neurons are 'mirroring' the neurons in the person's brain that is actually doing the act. Your neurons are firing in an attempt to understand and predict what the other person is doing and is going to do.

Here's the exciting part. If you pick up that glass and throw it against a wall, the firing pattern that happens when you are *picking up the glass* will be different than if you *intend* to take a drink. In both cases, taking a drink or throwing the glass against the wall, the part when you are picking up the glass is the same. But the neurons in your brain are firing a different pattern while you are picking up the glass depending what you intend to do with it.

When you are watching someone else pick up a glass the firing pattern of your neurons depends on what you expect them to do with that glass. You are trying to interpret their intentions in advance. What does this mean? It means that what you believe and what you expect dictate the firing pattern of neurons in your brain in response to your environment.

The firing patterns of your neurons, which is happening all the time, is partially controlled by what you are seeing or experiencing and partially controlled by what you believe or expect. Your beliefs and expectations control the way your brain fires in response to your environment throughout the entire day, however insignificant the situation might seem.

How does this affect the future? You will attend to things that support your beliefs and filter out things that don't. Your beliefs will dictate the way you respond to opportunities. If you have empowering beliefs that allow your brain to focus on the positive opportunity in your environment you will act very differently than if you have disempowering beliefs that will force your brain to focus on the risk and danger. This is how your beliefs affect the future. They effect how you behave every day.

The place you are at today is a compilation of all of the decisions you have made in the past. What may have seemed like small decisions, maybe even split second reactions, have had an impact on where you are now. These decisions were all grounded in the beliefs that you held at that time. This is why I say that we should do everything we can to teach our children to adopt empowering beliefs. Those that will cause them to find opportunity and react in a way that will take them forward, not in a way that will hold them back.

Believe it—Recap

I hope you have gained a unique perspective from reading this chapter and had some thoughts of your own. Here is a recap of the main points from this chapter.

- You don't know what you don't know so don't assume you always have the right answer.
- There is no reason to have disempowering beliefs when you can choose empowering ones instead.
- Finding your own voice and helping your kids to find theirs will promote their ability to contribute value to their world and achieve their own dreams.

ACTion™ plan

The final action plan of this book will help you promote empowering beliefs in yourself and your kids so that they may seek to fulfill their potential. To get the most out of the plan you can download the Action Guide at http://www.thebraincode.com/ActionGuide. As in the last chapter, these concepts will be very individualized and the specific steps will leave a lot of room for you to modify it to for your own unique situation.

1. **Assess your own beliefs and those you promote in your kids**
   - Evaluate your own beliefs. Do you have beliefs relating to yours or your kids' abilities that are holding you back?
   - Do you hold disempowering beliefs that might not be true?
   - Are there empowering beliefs that you could replace them with?
2. **Commit to empowering your kids**
   - Don't allow the words 'I can't' without challenging them. Whenever your kids use these words, probe them and ask them why they believe that. Get them to evaluate their own beliefs in their own mind.
   - Get revenge for all of the 'why' questions they threw at you when they were 2 years old. Throw the 'why' questions back at them to get them to think about any disempowering beliefs.
   - Help them find a different perspective to adopt an empowering belief instead.
3. **Track your progress and celebrate success**
   - Reassess your beliefs after a month of trying to stay conscious of them. This will require a greater degree of introspection since this is much less measurable than endpoints in the other section plans.

- Have you changed your perspective on anything? Have you noticed any changes in the way your kids respond to situations?
- Have you replaced any disempowering beliefs with empowering ones?

The final chapter of this book will bring all the previous ones together.

CHAPTER 8
PUT IT ALL TOGETHER —MAXIMIZE BRAIN POWER

This brings us to the last chapter. Why did I choose to focus on the topics I did? Hopefully, by now you realize that these topics are all related because they all affect how our brains function. Working on the brain and body at the same time as the mind and spirit, benefits all of them.

The brain is the master integrator of everything we do and experience. It is the ultimate machine. By focusing on the brain, you will simultaneously optimize your body, mind and spirit as well. It all comes back to the brain in the end.

The first section of this book talked about using physical health as a way to build the infrastructure of your kids' brains. By paying attention to their diet, physical activity and sleep needs, you are giving them the raw materials that they require for optimal development. You are laying the foundation that will allow them to realize their intellectual and emotional potential.

I talked about how to use exercise to increase the performance of brain regions and pathways responsible for attention, responsiveness, and handling stress. I talked about how to use nutrition to supply the raw materials to build pathways and protect against today's environmental threats. I also talked about how sleep regulates our biological rhythms and how you can use it to control many functions, including fat storage, growth and learning.

In the second section I talked about building upon the infrastructure created by the habits of section one. You learned how giving your kids experience in different environments promotes adaptability. You learned how to fill their minds with creative and empowering thoughts to promote independence.

In the end, it's all about optimization. What are the chances that your kids will reach their potential and achieve their goals and dreams? The more you pay attention to the topics detailed in this book, the better odds you give them. Do you want them to be ahead of the curve right now or behind it? Do you want them to continue good health and clear thinking into their older years or decay with those that ignored these issues? Will they create a life of happiness and pleasure or disappointment and pain? These questions may seem provocative but the answers largely depend on the actions you take today.

I hope you also realize that in order best help your kids you need to role model these lifestyle choices as well. It is much easier to help your kids when you are working from a position of credibility, demonstrating the choices you are trying to instill.

If you have ever flown in an airplane, you have heard the flight attendant talking about how oxygen masks will appear in case of a drop in cabin pressure. What is the instruction that he or she gives? "Put your own mask on first before assisting your children." Many financial planners will give you similar advice when talking about saving for a college education. They will tell you to attend to your own financial health with the appropriate retirement and savings plans and then contribute to your children's college fund.

Why is this advice so important? You are in a much better position to help your kids if you are working from a position of strength. The same is true for the topics discussed in this book. It is much better to help your kids with their diet and physical activity if you have a good plan yourself. It is much easier to get them to bed on time if you are not 'burning the candle at both ends' yourself. It is also much easier to help them seek new experiences, think independently and believe in themselves if they see these behaviors from you. I wrote this book for a parent's perspective to help their kids but all of the approaches are applicable to adults as well.

I sincerely hope that you found the content of this book useful. I hope that I have given you the motivation to be proactive about physical and mental health. If you were already proactive, I hope that I have given you the drive to stay the course, and have given you some different perspectives on how to do that. I hope that as you finish this book you don't just go back to doing the same old things but that you identify the areas where you can improve and take action immediately to do something about it.

I encourage you to contribute your own stories, experiences and motivators at http://www.thebraincode.com/brainblog. You can enter comments in the ongoing discussion pages to add your own advice. As I said in the beginning of the book, we all come to parenting from a unique perspective. We are all in this together. The more our kids can positively influence the world the better it is for all of us.

Any successful person will tell you that accountability to someone was a key factor in his or her accomplishments. Most people simply don't have the discipline to be accountable to themselves and go it alone. We need to have someone else there, keeping our momentum going. I have had many mentors in my own life to help me move forward. Some were informal through relationships with family and friends. Others were formal through school, sports or professional mentoring programs.

I sincerely want you to succeed in your goals to move yourself and your children to a position of strong physical and mental health. For best results, I strongly encourage you to make yourself accountable to someone else. You can visit our website at http://www.thebraincode.com to learn about individualized or group programs that will take you to the next level.

Your kids are your dreams so feed them well.

ABOUT THE AUTHOR

Simon was born to British parents in England. He grew up in Seattle, Washington after his father accepted a job with the Boeing Airplane Company. When Simon was in kindergarten, his teacher told his parents that he was going to be a scientist—she was right.

After high school, Simon earned a B.S. in Biology and then a PhD in Molecular and Cellular Biology. Dr. Evans spent the last decade studying neuroscience and the effect of stress on the brain. However, with current U.S. trends of decaying health he has turned his attention to the interaction between nutrition, exercise and brain fitness. At the time of this writing, he was applying this focus as a research scientist in the Psychiatry Department at the University of Michigan.

In addition to Simon's scientific interests, he is an avid soccer player. Simon played competitive youth soccer, captained his college team and was an all conference college player. Simon has been volunteering his time as a youth soccer coach for the last two decades. He now coaches kids at several levels and holds a national coaching license.

Finally, and most importantly for this book, Simon is a parent. His scientific background gives him theoretical understanding of how the brain works, his coaching background gives him experience teaching kids, and his role as a parent makes him a realist. He knows what parents can realistically do in today's society and understands the dilemmas that they face.

Dr. Simon Evans lives with his wife and two children near Ann Arbor, Michigan.

CLAIM YOUR FREE BONUSES TODAY

The Purchase of this book entitles you to download the **Brain Fitness Action Guide** and all current *AND* future Podcasts from the Brain Code. Each time we add a new Podcast you can choose to be automatically notified.

- Download and print the Action Guide worksheets an UNLIMITED number of times.
- Listen to Professional Athletes, Chefs, Brain Scientists, Sports Trainers and more.
- Get a FREE subscription to the Brain Code Journal.

These offers are yours at no extra cost as a thank you for taking action to help your family with the information in this book. Together we can ensure a healthy and successful future.

Get Immediate Access to your Bonuses at http://www.thebraincode.com/ActionGuide.

Printed in the United States
73012LV00001B/136-156